Breaking Things at Work

Breaking Things at Work

*The Luddites Are Right about
Why You Hate Your Job*

Gavin Mueller

VERSO

London • New York

For Finn and Eve, my children.

First published by Verso 2021
© Gavin Mueller 2021

1 3 5 7 9 10 8 6 4 2

Verso
UK: 6 Meard Street, London W1F 0EG
US: 20 Jay Street, Suite 1010, Brooklyn, NY 11201
versobooks.com

Verso is the imprint of New Left Books

ISBN-13: 978-1-78663-677-5
ISBN-13: 978-1-78663-675-1 (UK EBK)
ISBN-13: 978-1-78663-676-8 (US EBK)

British Library Cataloguing in Publication Data
A catalogue record for this book is available from the British Library

Library of Congress Cataloging-in-Publication Data
A catalog record for this book is available from the Library of Congress
Library of Congress Control Number: 2020948684

Typeset in Sabon by MJ & N Gavan, Truro, Cornwall
Printed and bound by CPI Group (UK) Ltd, Croydon CR0 4YY

Contents

Acknowledgements

Writing this book has required a journey through three cities, two continents, multiple jobs and gigs, and even a spate of unemployment. This is to say that it, for better or for worse, is a product of academic precarity. As far as I know, all my subsequent work will be. And I also know first-hand how difficult it is to produce under such conditions: frantic bursts of overwork punctuated by stretches of debilitating underwork, uprooting from intellectual and social networks, the Sisyphean feeling of starting in a new place, yet again, from scratch. You lose track of people, they lose track of you. Plans and projects easily dissipate in such an atmosphere. I can only imagine the wonderful work that won't see the light of day due to these conditions. It is a fate that could have just as easily befallen this book.

The fact that I was able to produce this book is only due to the consistencies and continuities I was able to establish in my life. First, above all was my wife, Katie. Second, was my ongoing commitment to *Viewpoint Magazine*, where I concretized much of the perspective that marks this book: my resistance to teleological views of history and ontological accounts of class, my abiding interest in struggles from below and beyond official institutions and ideologies of the left. This is, I am confident saying, a very "Viewpoint" book in its theoretical and political commitments.

The Marxist intellectual tradition has never been content to rest on credentialed experts, but spreads its purview widely to all manner of homegrown theoreticians, hobbyist auto-didacts, zine-writing worker-militants, roving antinomian bohemians, and, yes, its share of university professors. This motley assemblage of intellectual production, its contentious and fragmentary unity, is one thing that makes Marxism so exciting to me, and in this book I have attempted to be true to the heterogeneity of its practitioners. To put it another way, I strive to be faithful to Marxism's heretical side, its unofficial channels and para-academic spaces, as in spite of my academic credentials, these are what have ultimately shaped me and my work. And so here, somewhat oddly for a book on Luddism, I'd like to acknowledge the vibrant corners of my social media networks that have made an indelible mark on this book, in particular the Relaxed Marxist Discussion Facebook group.

I would also like to acknowledge a few individuals signifi-cant in the genesis of this work. My erstwhile colleague at Dallas, Andrew Culp, provided important conversations and a leg up in the formalities of proposing a book. Lisa Furchgott provided me with crucial historical sources at an early stage. I would especially like to thank the patience and perspicacity of my editor at Verso Books, Ben Mabie, who stuck with me on this longer-than-expected journey.

Introduction

Jeff Bezos is going to the moon. In May of 2019, just a few blocks from the White House, he unveiled the lunar lander developed by his secretive Blue Origin space exploration company to the jaunty falsetto harmonies of Electric Light Orchestra's "Mr. Blue Sky." *New York Times* journalist Kenneth Chang likened the gala, dubbed the "Going to Space to Benefit Earth" event, to "the announcement of an iPhone." "We are going to build a road to space," the Amazon CEO vowed, extending a hand to the Trump administration's own ambitions to send astronauts to the moon. "And then amazing things will happen."[1] What kinds of things? Nothing short of planetary exodus: Bezos has an oft-stated vision of trillions of human beings floating in space on millions of massive cylindrical colonies. It's a dream that, like so many of those among Silicon Valley's elite, comes right out of old science fiction, in this case 1976's *High Frontier* by physicist Gerard K. O'Neil, a book that, upon its publication, inspired Congress to abandon all funding for space colonization.[2]

But, for Bezos, space colonies are serious business. Not because they can solve the intractable problems of Earth: global poverty and environmental degradation are mere "short-term" problems.[3] With Earth's supply of resources dwindling, the future of technological progress itself relies on drawing from the vast quantities of minerals locked away in distant celestial bodies. Humanity will have go along for the ride.

Of course, Bezos isn't the only billionaire betting big on outer space. Elon Musk's flashier SpaceX has its sights set on

Mars. Holding court on Twitter, as is his wont, he revealed plans to transport 100,000 travelers a year to the red planet—for a fee. And those who can't afford a ticket through the solar system can take out a loan and work it off at one of SpaceX's off-planet facilities.[4] For Musk, as for Bezos, space travel is not a profit-making endeavor; it is a project to restore faith in the future itself. "You want to wake up in the morning and think the future is going to be great, and that's what being a spacefaring civilization is all about," he proclaimed at the International Astronautical Congress in 2017. "It's about believing in the future and thinking that the future will be better than the past."[5]

Not all of our tech billionaires want to travel the spaceways, but they all share something in common (that is, aside from a propensity to dine with the late sex-trafficking financier Jeffrey Epstein). They believe that technology lays a path to a brighter future, that the progress of humanity is one and the same as the progress of machines and gizmos. Bill Gates wants to use computers to overhaul education, and genetically modified organisms to solve hunger in Africa; he also sponsors a competition to invent new toilets to address the lack of sanitation infrastructure in the global South. (The Gates Foundation recently granted a Goalkeepers Global Goals Award to India's right-wing prime minister, Narendra Modi, for his dedication to the toilet cause.) Mark Zuckerberg, to his credit, acknowledges some of the shortcomings of his own company. "I used to think that if we just gave people a voice and helped them connect, that would make the world better by itself. In many ways it has. But our society is still divided," he writes in, naturally, a Facebook post. "Now I believe we have a responsibility to do even more. It's not enough to simply connect the world, we must also work to bring the world closer together."[6] Never one for excessively creative thinking, Zuck argues that solving the problems exacerbated by Facebook requires, well, more Facebook.

Peter Thiel, Facebook board member and Musk's former PayPal partner, and now a venture capitalist with a taste for extreme-right libertarian politics, does not hesitate to reach for the supernatural register to explain his faith in technology: "Humans are distinguished from other species by our ability to work miracles. We call these miracles technology."[7] Such is his zeal for the promise of technologies like artificial intelligence and life extension that anyone who lacks it is suspicious. He aligns the nostalgic tastes of "hipsters" with the Unabomber Ted Kaczynski's "loss of faith in the technological frontier."[8]

In a more muted register, the Lolita Express–traveling Harvard psychologist Steven Pinker, who is something of a Dr. Pangloss of the Davos set, wants you to know you've never had it so good. In his 2018 *Enlightenment Now*, Pinker seeks to combat "progressophobia," an affliction caused by liberal arts intellectuals who assign Theodor Adorno and Jean-Paul Sartre to their young charges.[9] But, even as an avowed secularist, Pinker, like Thiel, can't help but reach for the cosmic. "Though I am skittish about any notion of historical inevitability, cosmic forces, or mystical arcs of justice, some kinds of social change really do seem to be carried along by an inexorable tectonic force."[10] This force may be the very milieu that props up his book sales, as he takes pains to celebrate "technophilanthropists," information technology, smartphones, online education, microfinance, and, at the risk of sounding redundant, Bill Gates himself, whose effusive praise graces the cover of the book. As Pinker brushes aside statistics on rising inequality, he warns his readers about the enemies of progress— environmentalists, Marxists, populists, and leftists: "The impression that the modern economy has left most people behind encourages Luddite ... policies," he cautions.[11]

While the technological optimism of billionaires comes from the political right and center, it can also be found on the radical left, where so-called accelerationists anticipate a fully automated luxury communism on the back of the wildest fantasies of Silicon Valley entrepreneurs, and the self-proclaimed "pro-science left" embrace the logistical organization of the most exploitative businesses on the planet. The accelerationists are, as they often point out, subscribing to a prevalent view from within the Marxist tradition. Historically, Marxists have not been critical of technology, even when that technology is deployed in the workplace in ways that seem detrimental for workers. For many Marxists, technology is at worst neutral: it is not the technology itself, but who controls it, labor or capital. And for some of them, technology, even when wielded by capitalists, is a boon to socialism, creating the conditions of radical transformation right under the bosses' noses. This means that a socialist movement should treat technological development, even if it has negative consequences in the short term, as something positive.

I disagree, both with the billionaires and with the pro-tech Marxists who are much closer to my own political and theoretical perspectives. In my view, technology often plays a detrimental role in working life, and in struggles for a better one. Technological development leads to vast accumulations of wealth, and with that, power, for the people who exploit workers. In turn, technology reduces the autonomy of workers —their ability to organize themselves to fight against their exploiters. It robs people of the feeling that they can control their own lives, that they can set the terms of their world. If you have an interest in the fates of these people, and count yourself as someone who wants a more egalitarian future than the current system can provide, you should be critical of technology, and acknowledge those moments where people, especially those at work, have resisted it.

This is to say that this is a book about Luddism. It is not a book about the Luddites, although I discuss them in the first chapter. Rather, I am interested in the politics behind the movement formed by the weavers of early nineteenth-century England, politics that took a militant stance toward the technological reorganization of work undertaken by early capitalists. The Luddites believed that new machines were undermining their livelihoods and destroying their communities, and that targeting those machines was a valid strategy in their fight against it. I believe that the terms of debate over work and the future of the economy in our current moment could benefit from such a perspective, along with a better understanding of how Luddism continued to traverse worker movements, up until the present day. It is, as we shall see, the irrepressible, if still unconscious, spirit of the twenty-first-century workplace.

One of my goals in writing this book is to turn Marxists into Luddites. I go about this in two ways. First, I excavate a strand of thought from within Marxist theory, going back to Marx himself, to demonstrate that Luddism is intellectually compatible with Marxism. But this project is not simply a philosophical endeavor. Rather, Marxist theory has to be put to the test of history, the test of the actual practices of workers themselves—those actions that inspired Marx's theorizations and the work of many of the best Marxists after him. And so I also recover important struggles where workers focused not only on their class antagonist (personified by bosses or managers), but on the machines deployed in this struggle as well. My argument boils down to this: to be a good Marxist is to also be a Luddite.

While I want to make Marxists into Luddites, I also have another goal: I want to turn people critical of technology into Marxists. If, as Marx argued, a society's ruling ideas are those of its ruling class, then technological optimism should indeed be at the top of the heap. And yet, our billionaires and their Ivy League hangers-on protest too much. Their blithe boosterism for optimism itself belies the fact that among those of less-than-astronomical means, technological optimism is on the wane. We are increasingly turning against the technologies that saturate our work and leisure, and I think there are powerful political possibilities here, but only if this perspective is connected to a larger critique of the social and economic system in which we live: capitalism. Marxist theory offers many important tools in understanding how capitalism works, and how it can be changed—tools I want to share with people who may not think of themselves as Marxists. In fact, I hope this book is accessible to people without much of a background in Marxist theory. Maybe it will be your introduction to an intellectual tradition as rich, varied, and scintillating as any I've encountered.

Much of our contemporary technological criticism comes from a place of romantic humanism, whether acknowledged or not, the notion that technology has separated us from some kind of essential part of ourselves, that it alienates us from what makes us really human. For example, social scientist and influential technology critic Sherry Turkle asks us to "reclaim conversation" from our smartphones, which alienate us from the "raw, human part" of our existence by allowing us to live in a convenient and curated reality.[12] In a similar register, Tim Wu concludes his fascinating history of media advertising, *The Attention Merchants*, with what he calls "a human reclamation project" to protect our attention from the techniques and technologies of the ad-driven internet. Wu extolls practices like "unplugging" as the beginnings of a larger endeavor "to make our attention our own again, and so reclaim ownership of the very experience of living."[13] In the complaints of Turkle and Wu, we might hear echoes of Martin Heidegger, who criticized technology for alienating us, through its disenchanting and instrumentalizing nature, from the mystical experience of Being.[14]

Even if I believed in a universal human essence (full disclosure: I do not), to recover it would not be enough. The problem of technology is not simply that it alienates us from Being, or from authentic experiences. After all, this is a problem for which the tech companies themselves are happy to sell the solution: Google and Apple have launched their own "well-being" services to help users cut back on screen time.[15] Instead, the more fundamental problem of technology is its role in the reproduction of hierarchies and injustices foisted upon most of us by business owners, bosses, and governments. In other words, the problem of technology is its role in capitalism. In this book, I aim to show how technology developed by capitalism furthers its goals: it compels us to work more, limits our autonomy, and outmaneuvers and divides us when we organize to fight back. In response, a flourishing class struggle will necessarily target the machines of the day, and I document the moments where it has.

In this way, I am not simply lobbing advice at movements by telling them to go out and break machines. What I try to do is show that *workers themselves* have repeatedly become Luddites in struggle. This was true of the self-proclaimed followers of King Ludd of the early nineteenth century, and it is true of workers down through the decades since. It is even true of some of the most technologically adept workers of the computer age. If Marxists should do anything, it is to study and learn from the history of past struggles, to recover the voices from past movements so that they might inform current ones. Our theory should take its form from these struggles, not advise and chastise them from on high.

When I started writing this book, my position was not a popular one. Accelerationism was having its time in the sun, with its belief, in both its right- and left-wing guises, that exponential technological development could surmount the political and social impasses of our current moment. Its gambit was that we could take a cybernetic leap out of late neoliberalism's doldrums. But the tenor has changed. After 2016, fewer people than ever have faith in the future, and still fewer believe in the salutary effects of the latest developments in digital networks, automation, or artificial intelligence. "Twitter revolutions" in the Middle East have been ground into dust.

The cheap scooters of the so-called sharing economy choke our streets, and we collectively celebrate their destruction on the Instagram account Bird Graveyard. There is a palpable rise in Luddite sentiments, as well as anti-capitalist ones. As the following chapters show, these attitudes complement each other, and hold the key to the future of radical politics.

1

The Nights of King Ludd

In the second decade of the nineteenth century, the British Crown faced a problem. Discontented weavers, croppers, and other textile workers had begun a protracted insurgency against property and the state. At issue were new types of machines —the stocking frame, the gig mill, and the shearing frame— that could produce and finish cloth using a fraction of the labor time previously required, transforming a skilled profession into low-grade piecework. Wages plummeted and hunger began to set in. Communities of thousands were threatened by the upheaval.

Some of these technologies had floated around England and France for centuries, repeatedly drawing the anger of workers. Croppers had been targeting gig mills, in particular, for years: as the eighteenth century came to a close, several mills in Leeds had been publicly destroyed. (Subsequent investigations by authorities tellingly failed to find any witnesses to the events.) In some cases, weavers successfully appealed to prior government decisions protecting their livelihoods from technology. However, after just a few years, the situation was rapidly changing. Parliament's preoccupation with the wars against Napoleon meant it had little patience for the demands of unruly craftsmen. The new Combination Laws, which outlawed trade union activity, severely limited collective action by textile weavers. Mill owners saw an opportunity, and redoubled their efforts to introduce machines and reduce wages. As tensions intensified, a new strategy emerged.

Between 1811 and 1812, hundreds of new frameworks were destroyed in dozens of coordinated, clandestine attacks under the aegis of a mythical leader called "Ned Ludd." In addition to their notorious raids, the so-called Luddites launched vociferous public protests, sparked chaotic riots, and continually stole from mills—activities all marked by an astonishing level of organized militancy. Their politics not only took the form of violent activity but was also enunciated through voluminous decentralized letter-writing campaigns, which petitioned—and sometimes threatened—local industrialists and government bureaucrats, pressing for reforms such as higher minimum wages, cessation of child labor, and standards of quality for cloth goods. The Luddites' political activities earned them the sympathies of their communities, whose widespread support protected the identities of militants from the authorities. At the height of their activity in Nottingham, from November 1811 to February 1812, disciplined bands of masked Luddites attacked and destroyed frames almost every night. Mill owners were terrified. Wages rose.

The weaver insurrection threatened to link up with other underground anti-government currents, such as the Jacobins—indeed, at least one Luddite signed his letter with the name of the recently deceased republican writer Thomas Paine. Parliament was now sufficiently interested. It dispatched soldiers across the country to quell the violence and passed new legislation that made frame breaking a capital offense. The poet Lord Byron gave his first speech to Parliament denouncing these measures leveled against the Luddite "mob." "You may call the people a mob, but do not forget that a mob too often speaks the sentiments of the people," he warned.[1] As if to acknowledge Byron's point, small mill owners were increasingly afraid to implement the machines. This also meant that owners of the larger workshops that continued to use frames knew they were likely targets.

William Cartwright was one such owner, and he was prepared for the inevitable Luddite attack. On the night of April 9,

1812, the Luddites had launched a daring raid on the massive Horbury mill complex owned by Joseph Foster, assembling a force of hundreds to successfully wreck and burn the building, after detaining Foster's sons without bloodshed. Cartwright wouldn't be so easy a mark. He had fortified his mill and holed up inside with several militia members. When, on April 11, the Luddites descended on his factory and began to smash apart the door with hammers, he and his men opened fire. After a gun battle, the Luddites retreated, leaving behind two wounded men who later succumbed to their injuries. In spite of intense surveillance and investigation, none of the attackers were identified, even after a series of assassination attempts on mill owners (one successful) at the end of April.

Yet eventually the spies and crackdowns had their effect, and in January 1813 authorities identified, arrested, and executed several suspected Luddite higher-ups. The most pronounced phase of machine breaking rapidly subsided. But the movement lived on in the underground, bolstered by a powerful mythology and its storied confrontation with the detested state. Sporadic outbreaks of machine breaking continued for years. It was this quality Lord Byron captured in "Song for the Luddites," his 1816 encomium to the movement, which portrayed it as heroically doomed, but successful at laying the groundwork for future emancipatory struggles. The blood shed by the Luddites was "the dew / Which the tree shall renew / Of Liberty, planted by Ludd!"[2] This mythological, subterranean character has carried forward to our own time; as E.P. Thompson says, "To this day Luddism refuses to give up all its secrets."[3]

In spite of Byron's efforts, history has not been kind to the Luddites. Their militant opposition to machines has meant that their legacy has been understood as a kind of technophobia. And because their rebellion occurred during the early days of the advent of mass production, the Luddites have become synonymous with an irrational fear of inevitable progress. Critics of technology find themselves either performatively disclaiming the Luddite legacy or professing their unbecoming sympathies. "I'm not a Luddite," insists technology writer Andrew Keen while explaining his antipathy toward social media,[4] just as "Luddite confessionals" have become an established essay genre, encompassing educators, musicians, and even information technology professionals.[5]

The Luddites' association with technophobia has itself garnered them vocal sympathizers. In 1984, Thomas Pynchon dryly inquired whether it was "O.K. to be a Luddite,"[6] and the nineties saw the so-called neo-Luddite movement, which brought together sundry social critics with radical environmentalists in a loose coalition opposed to contemporary technologies. While their manifesto specified that they did not oppose technology as such, the neo-Luddites' opposition to everything from genetic engineering to television, computers, and "electromagnetic technologies" belied a debt to anticivilization anarcho-primitivist politics.[7] Odd tics, such as an identification with Unabomber Ted Kaczynski[8] and the subsequent flirtations of leading figure (and author of an evocative history of the Luddites) Kirkpatrick Sale with secession movements,[9] give off a distinct odor of crankishness.

It is the nature of myths to contain an element of flexibility and indeterminacy in their application. Indeed, the Luddites assumed a mythic character in their own time: they invoked the name of an imaginary king. The construction of a mythos, tied to a collective subject, is part of what has made the Luddite struggle a common turn of phrase 200 years after the fact. As media theorist Marco Deseriis argues, the rhetorical power of the Luddites lay in their articulation of otherwise loosely connected struggles into a set of linked practices and narratives, what he calls an "assemblage of enunciation": "a network of pragmatic actions and semiotic expressions that are connected but also enjoy relative autonomy." The function of the "improper name" of Ned Ludd is, according to Deseriis, "precisely to eschew fixation by incorporating a plurality of usages that cannot easily be reduced to one."[10]

After all, the Luddites were not the first instance of an organized attack on industrial manufacturing: stocking frames, specifically, had been targeted for decades, and the British Parliament had passed an act protecting the machines in 1788. The wealthy and powerful understood machines as a method to accumulate power, and so too did the toiling classes over whom they wished to exert it. And so destruction and sabotage accompanied the introduction of machines wherever they were introduced. Marx notes the protracted hostility to wind- and waterpower stretching back to at least the 1630s.[11] Industrial machines inspired a special ire, as they not only disrupted traditional ways of life, but brutally ground down their workers. London's massive Albion Mills, the probable inspiration for William Blake's line about "dark Satanic mills," was burned to the ground in 1791—possibly at the hands of its workers, who cheered the blaze from the riverbanks of the Thames while ignoring authorities' pleas to help fight the fire. Satirists of the day were quick to label the celebrants dangerous radicals and partisans for outdated machines.[12] In 1805 French silk weavers greeted the arrival of the Jacquard loom by attempting to assassinate its inventor and destroying the device publicly in Lyon.[13] After the brief flourishing of the Luddite rebellions, destruction of machines and factories continued in France, in the United States (where a number of textile factories went up in flames, likely from arson), and throughout Silesia and Bavaria.[14]

In light of a history rife with workers destroying machines, why do the Luddites cast the longest shadow? It is not only because they knew how to spin a good yarn. After all, the Crown doesn't muster a military force of thousands to destroy a myth. The Luddites loom large because of the power of their struggle, both in literature and in their historical accomplishments. While E.P. Thompson has sought to rescue the Luddites from "the enormous condescension of posterity" through an act of radical sympathy, he still acknowledged that militant reactions against industrialism "may have been foolhardy. But they lived through these times of acute social disturbance, and we did not."[15] I admire Thompson's ability to comprehend the Luddites from within their specific conjuncture, rather than from a point of view that sees them as a mere speed bump on the road to our inevitable present.

But we can go further. History has a shape, but it is not one that is foretold, still less one forecast by the tools and technologies at hand. Instead, the shape of history, as Marx argued, is wrought by the struggles of those who participated in it. That the Luddites were ultimately unsuccessful is not itself an indictment: final success is a poor criterion for judging an action before or during the fact. And, as I hope to demonstrate, Luddism was not altogether pointless. Our history is the Luddites' as well, and their insight—that technology was political, and that it could and, in many cases, should be opposed—has carried down through all manner of militant movements, including those of the present. There is much to learn from this tradition, even among the most technophilic current-day radicals.

The Luddite opposition to machines was, it must be said, not a simple technophobia. As Sale notes, many of the Luddites were weavers or other skilled textile workers who operated their own complicated tools.[16] Their revolt was not against machines in themselves, but against the industrial society that threatened their established ways of life, and of which machines were the chief weapon. To say they fought machines makes about as much sense as saying a boxer fights against fists. As Sale describes it, the Luddite rebellions were never simply against technology, but "what that machinery stood for: the palpable, daily evidence of their having to succumb to forces beyond their control."[17]

Machine breaking was only one technique among many that the Luddites deployed, reserved for use against the most intransigent factory owners as part of a wider strategy to increase worker power.[18] Weavers invoked King Ludd in their attempts to collectively bargain for piece rates that would allow them to survive, and in their petitions to government authorities for redress. One letter sent to the Home Office in 1812, signed "Ned Lud's Office, Sherwood Forest," stated that "all frames of whatsoever discription the worckmen of which Are not paid in the current Coin of the realm will Invarioably be distroy'd," while vowing to protect the frames of compliant owners.[19]

Historian Eric Hobsbawm, in a reevaluation of the Luddites' motivations for machine breaking, describes them as "collective bargaining by riot." For Hobsbawm, "The value of this technique was obvious, both as a means of putting pressure on employers, and of ensuring the essential solidarity of the workers."[20] Machine breaking was one weapon among many, but it was also a technique for something else: forging a shared communal struggle. Hobsbawm views this practice as entirely appropriate for the early nineteenth century. "In those presocialist times the working class was a crowd, not an army," he writes. "Enlightened, orderly, bureaucratic strikes were impossible."[21]

Here, Hobsbawm suggests the most important element of the Luddites: his analysis reorients the discussion away from the movement's quixotic outcome and toward an emphasis on *class composition*. The concept of class composition, an effort to grasp class in both its economic and political dimensions in tandem, was developed by Italian theorists like Raniero Panzieri, Sergio Bologna, and Mario Tronti to account for the new forms of resistance exhibited by the youthful "mass workers," deskilled by the introduction of new machinery into factories.[22] Class composition, then, is a rebuke to the notion of class as a preexisting empirical category—an idea you might encounter in a basic sociology textbook, where you simply look at someone's job or income and determine their class.

Rather, class in the Marxist sense is forged through struggle itself. As the writers of 1970s journal *Zerowork* put it, "For us, as Marx long ago, the working class is defined by its struggle against capital and not [merely] by its productive function."[23]

In Hobsbawm's estimation, the working-class activity of the Luddites has to be understood in terms of its existing technical composition; indeed, workers had not yet been organized into a disciplined mass, but were instead a mélange of laborers working in their own homes and shops, often with their own tools. Physically separated and without established organizations, they often related to bosses according to individualized contracts, and so it was impossible for them to engage in the kinds of militancy we associate with trade unions made up of mass workers. But Hobsbawm suggests something further: that through machine breaking itself, the Luddites *composed themselves as a class* by creating bonds of solidarity.

This is not exactly to use, in the Hegelian version of Marx's analysis, the vocabulary of an empirical "class in itself" transforming into a politicized "class for itself"—terms never deployed by Marx himself. As historian Salar Mohandesi notes, while writers such as Thompson have used this vocabulary to explain class beyond a vulgar economic reduction, it leaves little room for the sudden emergence of struggle and ties these struggles too closely to a discrete cultural way of life.[24] Instead, we can think about the actions of the Luddites, and other machine breaking, as *practices of political composition*. Workers are organized and exploited according to their technical composition; they then develop the forms of struggle necessary for overcoming their divisions and fighting their exploitation.

In the case of the Luddites, these were largely independent workers resisting their incorporation into the factory while fighting for the preservation of other elements of their way of life and their communities. They could not compose themselves in the way mass workers might, and they did not limit their struggle to the workplace. Instead, the class composed itself around a collective mythical subject—King Ludd—and forged practices of secrecy and community-wide solidarity in order to keep the struggle alive and protect its direct participants. These practices extended into secret oaths, bonds of confidentiality —authorities struggled to get Luddites to inform on their comrades—and literary practices such as writing songs, poems, and letters. The organized attack on and destruction of factory machinery was not an isolated strategy, but was the very texture of struggle, the tissue holding together the weavers as a class. It was a practice of solidarity.

It is just this point that labor historian Peter Linebaugh seizes upon in his pamphlet *Ned Ludd and Queen Mab*. In thinking about the politics of machine breaking as a form of solidarity —a means of class composition—Linebaugh knits together a host of disparate yet contemporaneous struggles connected to the onslaught of primitive accumulation of the early nineteenth century. Capitalism was erected on a series of enclosures spanning the globe, a disruptive process of ordering and disciplining life and the means to sustain it. "The world was being enclosed," he writes. "Life was being closed off, people were being shut in."[25] The Luddites, fighting against the enclosure of their skills by "Machinery hurtful to Commonality," occupied only one front in a massive global struggle breaking out along a cotton commodity chain that stretched across the ocean, encompassing simultaneous rebellions by indigenous peoples and slaves in the New World. In these rebellions, attacks on productive technology were a common tactic. Insurgent Creeks destroyed the looms of their accommodationist peers that represented the new forms of trade accompanying the encroachment of the plantation economy.[26] And in the plantation fields, where the cotton originated, slaves broke their tools so often that owners "bought extra-heavy implements in the hope they would survive rough handling," thereby reducing the plantation economy's productivity.[27] As Linebaugh argues,

"The destruction of farm implements by those working them on American plantations belongs to the story of Luddism, not just because they too were tool-breakers, but they were part of the Atlantic recomposition of textile labor-power."[28] There is, he suggests, a germ of a shared endeavor in these aligned struggles against a common foe.

Marx and the Luddites

The rehabilitation of the Luddite legacy may be an important part of contemporary historiography, but what relevance does it have for struggles against capitalism? Here we should turn to Marx, capitalism's greatest analyst and critic, and other radical writers living through the momentous technological changes in production during the nineteenth century.

Machine breaking bewildered and frustrated many nineteenth-century bourgeois observers. Andrew Ure, whose 1835 *Philosophy of Manufactures* provided Marx with much of his knowledge of factory machines, declared that "cotton-spinners in particular have been so blinded by prejudice and passion" that they could not see the immense economic improvement of the nation brought about by stocking frames.[29] Political economist David Ricardo, another influential figure in Marx's thought, initially argued that the introduction of machines was a general good, though later he was forced to admit that "the substitution of machinery for human labour, is often very injurious to the interests of the class of labourers."[30]

But what did Marx himself say about technology? The history of Marxist thought and politics is littered with controversy over this question. The floridness of Marx's writing and the inaccessibility of his dialectical presentation have produced a host of ambiguities for Marxist theories of technology, further complicated by the way his project has been taken as doctrinal gospel rather than as setting up a wide-reaching agenda for radical inquiry. Viewed as a whole, it is difficult not to detect a distinct ambivalence in Marx's writing on technology.

There is evidence for a technophilic Marx. The old man was certainly fascinated by technology, writing about and researching it extensively, sketching new inventions as part of his study. Sometimes an enthusiasm for technology is thought to be an expression of begrudging admiration for the bourgeoisie, often joined by a larger claim that capitalism is a necessary stage on the path to socialism. After all, the *Communist Manifesto*, written during the revolutionary year of 1848, declares:

> Modern bourgeois society, with its relations of production, of exchange and of property, a society that has conjured up such gigantic means of production and of exchange, is like the sorcerer who is no longer able to control the powers of the nether world whom he has called up by his spells.[31]

In fact, Marx refers to these modern productive forces as "the weapons with which the bourgeoisie felled feudalism to the ground"—weapons that, once wielded by the proletariat, will be "turned against the bourgeoisie itself." This seems to indicate that Marx believed that the technologies developed by the bourgeoisie could be the groundwork for a future socialism, once the workers are in charge.

In later writing, Marx distinguishes between the social relations of production (the way human beings relate to one another, through class antagonism) and the technical relations of production (the way human beings relate to machines). In making this distinction, many have assumed that Marx bracketed technology off from the exploitative class system at the heart of capitalism, therefore suggesting that a socialist society would consist of a victorious working class's assumption of the mantle of an intact capitalist productive system. Marx's most technologically determinist passage from his preface to

A Contribution to the Critique of Political Economy seems to go even further. Here, he suggests that an exploitative class system will actually *impede* technological development, provoking revolution:

> At a certain stage of development, the material productive forces of society come into conflict with the existing relations of production or—this merely expresses the same thing in legal terms—with the property relations within the framework of which they have operated hitherto. From forms of development of the productive forces these relations turn into their fetters. Then begins an era of social revolution.[32]

As sociologist Donald MacKenzie notes, however, to interpret this passage as technologically determinist requires a faulty assumption: that Marx's use of "forces of production" is equivalent to "technology," rather than inclusive of human labor power.[33]

But while many readers of Marx have interpreted "productive forces" as the equivalent to technology, MacKenzie points out that human labor power—including its skills, abilities, techniques, and, most importantly, its conscious application—is also a force of production. If productive forces are understood correctly, as an *assemblage* of technology and people, what is fettered is not technological development itself, but a relationship between worker and machine in which the worker has conscious agency.

As Mackenzie rightly states, the "Preface" isn't Marx's most developed thinking on technology. A number of other commentators, in particular the technophilic authors associated with post-operaismo such as Antonio Negri and Carlo Vercellone, point, instead, to the so-called "Fragment on Machines" from the *Grundrisse*, Marx's notebooks on which he worked in preparation for writing *Capital*. In the "Fragment," Marx seems to sketch a future of fully automated production, "an automatic system of machinery,"[34] perhaps even a Fully Automated Luxury Communism driven by a "general intellect"—an assemblage of accumulated technical knowledge that could be an anticipation of the digital networks of the internet. According to Marx, the development of the productive forces reaches a level in which "it is the machine which possesses skill and strength in place of the worker, is itself the virtuoso."[35] In this arrangement, the worker "merely transmits the machine's work, the machine's action, on to the raw material—supervises it and guards against interruptions."[36]

During the economic restructuring of the 1980s and '90s, the "Fragment" seemed increasingly prescient of the knowledge economy of what Italian sociologist Maurizio Lazzarato called "immaterial laborers"—those who coordinate, communicate and create, rather than simply operate machines.[37] Machines take over physical production, while human beings focus on creativity and collaboration, educating themselves to acquire new skills and capacities. For Negri and his collaborator Michael Hardt, this self-valorizing and self-organizing character of immaterial labor implies an egalitarian future: "Immaterial labor thus seems to provide the potential for a kind of spontaneous and elementary communism."[38] Similarly, contemporary accelerationists such as Paul Mason and Aaron Bastani continue to refer to the passage as a harbinger to a future utopia.[39]

Yet, such a focus on this portion of the *Grundrisse* neglects key developments in Marx's concepts incorporated into the published work of *Capital*. Following the recommendation of Michael Heinrich, who points out that Marx had not yet refined his concepts,[40] let's look to the section of *Capital* where Marx returns to these questions, and where he deals more fully with the imbrication of machine and worker. Here, in Chapter 15, Marx has worked out a different theory of machines. Again, machinery appears as a weapon, but one of a different type:

It is the most powerful weapon for suppressing strikes, those periodic revolts of the working class against the autocracy of capital ... It would be possible to write a whole history of the inventions made since 1830 for the sole purpose of providing capital with weapons against working-class revolt.[41]

But Marx's most developed writing on technology comes from an unpublished chapter of *Capital* called "Results of the Immediate Production Process," which he had once intended as the conclusion of the first volume.[42] Here Marx contrasts two ways that capital controls the production process, with implications for the technology involved. The first, "formal" subsumption, "is only formally distinct from earlier modes of production ... either when the producer is self-employing or when the immediate producers are forced to deliver surplus labour for others."[43] In formal subsumption, independent craft laborers, such as the weavers who made up the Luddite rebellions, work for capitalists, who own the means of production. However, control over the labor process is delegated to the workers, who carry on as they had when they themselves owned their tools. "Technologically speaking," he writes, "the labour process goes on as before, with the proviso that it is now subordinated to capital."[44]

Under the second form, "real" subsumption, capital restructures the labor process itself by introducing machines and other technologies: "A complete revolution takes place in the mode of production itself, in the productivity of the workers and in the relations between workers and capitalists."[45] Here, as Marx describes, "the *labour process itself* is no more than the instrument of the *valorization process*." In other words, the practices and technologies of work center on the production of exchange value for profit, without any necessary connection to the usefulness of the goods, still less any "progress" in the quality of life for the worker, who is "a mere means of production."[46] As sociologist Nicholas Thoburn puts it, technology is thus "a means of consolidating a particular form of the extraction of value. The forces of production thus had capitalist relations immanent to them."[47] Marx lists some of the more destructive aspects of real subsumption: "production for production's sake," overproduction, and the creation of a surplus population unnecessary to existing production.[48]

At times, Marx appears to imply that formal subsumption is a historical stage prior to real subsumption. This would mean that there is a kind of telos to technology of production of which any kind of Marxist politics must take heed. But a careful reading, both of Marx and history, reveals that there is no necessary passage in production from one to another. In the communist theory collective Endnotes' summation, "If the categories of subsumption are applicable to history at all, this can therefore only be in a 'nonlinear' fashion: they cannot apply simplistically or unidirectionally to the historical development of the class relation."[49] Philosopher Patrick Murray argues that "Marx considers the possibility of a distinct historical stage of merely formal subsumption but finds no evidence of one";[50] instead, as Marx states of formal subsumption, "it is a particular form alongside the developed mode of production which is specifically capitalist."[51] Jan Breman's ethnographic work on the interpenetration of the formal and informal sector in Gujarat, India, is one chief example. There, the formal sector of really subsumed factories and mills relies upon the informal sector for inputs like bricks and raw materials, just as the advanced technology of Silicon Valley is built with rare earth metals mined "artisanally" by children using primitive tools.[52]

A teleological perspective that sees formal and real subsumption as subsequent "stages" of capitalist development presumes that capitalist development tends inexorably toward real subsumption, and therefore deskilling and automation, and that any kind of communism would be of the fully automated variety. It thus imposes a postwork futurism on Marx that his mature work does not support. In fact, it was Marx's political and intellectual rival, Pierre-Joseph Proudhon, who treated mechanization as inevitable and ultimately desirable. Exhorting workers to be "more attentive to the teachings of destiny," he insisted that while the immediate effects of capitalist technology would be disastrous, in the end it would lead to greater productivity and abundance: "The guarantee of our liberty lies in the progress of our torture."[53]

Marx himself makes some dismissive remarks about the "crude form" of the revolts of the Luddites. "It took both time and experience before the workers learnt to distinguish between machinery and its employment by capital, and therefore to transfer their attacks from the material instruments of production to the form of society which utilizes those instruments."[54] But one of the cornerstones of Marx's own view of radical practice, and what made him reluctant throughout his life to make programmatic and tactical arguments about a future egalitarian society, was his conviction that communism was "not a state of affairs which is to be established, an ideal to which reality [will] have to adjust itself." Rather, communism is "the real movement which abolishes the present state of things."[55] It is this perspective of Marx—not as a designer of a future society, nor even as a theoretician of the necessary grounds for socialism, but as a cartographer of proletarian struggle —that we should hold on to in our present moment. The struggles against machines *were* the struggles against the society that utilized them, and, moreover, these struggles had a number of important effects on the composition of the working class. In keeping an eye on our future technological society, we've taken it off the one thing that mattered above all else to Marx: what kinds of struggles people were making against capitalism, and the knowledge and experience these struggles have bequeathed to us.

I offer an example. Historian Michelle Perrot documents the manifold resistance to industrialization in France, where weaver struggles played out differently than in Britain, the site of Marx's investigations. Perrot argues that opposition to mechanization of the labor process, which included slowdowns, absenteeism, and sabotage, was a crucial component of resistance to a "producerist" vision of society and its work ethic. Workers encountered mechanization as both the extension of toil and the imposition of an entire worldview that valorized it. The legacy of this resistance has left a mark on French culture ever since. "Always ready to praise idleness, the French populace has a taste for games and wastefulness that has been deplored by employers and economists alike," she comments wryly.[56]

According to Perrot, the weavers' opposition to mechanization was not total opposition to industrialization, as workers often adopted elements of new cotton-spinning technologies to suit their work processes. For example, English weavers complained that bosses refused to implement "racks," devices that accurately measured productivity, and therefore secured workers' piece-rate wages. What workers bitterly opposed was "industrial concentration" that demolished their way of life by undermining the autonomy they possessed in small-scale home-based manufacturing, which "paced its activities according to its needs" so that workers controlled the hours and intensity of their work.[57]

Remarkably, the widespread popular resistance to mechanization in France succeeded, for a time. Factories went bankrupt, and home-based production predominated, though capitalists never fully conceded defeat, and they ultimately prevailed in erecting factories after a series of economic crises crippled the weavers. Other industries, such as sheep shearing, could only mechanize with assistance from the state. Perrot reminds us that the introduction of technology was, as Marx described it, a weapon in struggle: "Mechanization took place not merely because of technical or economic necessities but because of conflicts of authority."[58] Because this entrenched resistance was rooted in a style of work that did not separate the production of goods from the reproductive activities of the household and neighborhood, it greeted all manner of reorganization of daily life, from the advent of mass housing to streetlights, with hostility. Workers went on strike (or simply stopped showing up), took frequent breaks and even got drunk on the job. The entire community of Houlme rioted when the dinner hour was reduced to thirty minutes. Police were required to force textile workers to move to new "modern" accommodations closer to factories. Protests often incorporated community rituals, such as charivari, where effigies of offending authorities were paraded through towns and burned.[59] Struggle against capitalism was thus not only a fight in the workplace but overflowed into a politicization of technology in everyday life. For instance, "in 1848, the Paris insurgents destroyed lampposts, symbols of the eye of the police."[60]

Marxism-Morrisism

We can find echoes of the French craft workers' opposition to machines as instruments of toil, rather than the liberation of work, in the writings of William Morris, the English designer and socialist. Morris believed, as the poet Clive Wilmer puts it, that "under capitalism, machines were primarily used to increase production, thereby increasing the worker's drudgery."[61] Rather than churn out endless quantities of cheap goods, society should focus on goods' quality, which would not only reduce workloads but make work itself more pleasant. While he favored the use of machinery to reduce working hours, Morris's ideal of socialism was similarly qualitative, consisting of what he called "worthy work," which "carries with it the hope of pleasure in rest, the hope of the pleasure in our using what it makes, and the hope of pleasure in our daily creative skill."[62]

Morris thus differed from the many socialists of his day who advocated for increased leisure and rest in the form of reduced working hours. In his view, this was insufficient. It was not that Morris subscribed to a Protestant work ethic that valued work for its own sake. Rather, Morris's position was rooted in an understanding of Marx's dictum that the realm of freedom begins where the realm of necessity ends, and that necessity "will not be finally conquered till our work becomes a part of the pleasure of our lives"[63]—that is, until we find our work rewarding. A fundamental element of this "attractive work" was its reliance on the development of skill in the worker, which would allow the laborer "to take a pleasurable interest in all the details of life."[64] But such attractive work would require a dramatic rethinking of machines.

For Morris, the industrial system did not produce abundance, but existed merely for profit, and he recognized that a really subsumed productive process was irrevocably attached to "the necessity for grinding profits out of men's lives and of producing cheap goods for the use (and subjection) of the slaves who grind."[65] Capitalism required this kind of production, but socialism did not; moreover, the factory system was not to be assumed as a given in the new society, but needed to be questioned along with every other element of the organization of work. Bereft of the needs of profits and competition, many machines would be seen for the destroyers of life and pleasurable work that previous struggles, such as those of the Luddites, recognized:

> They are called "labour-saving" machines—a commonly used phrase which implies what we expect of them; but we do not get what we expect. What they really do is to reduce the skilled labourer to the rank of the unskilled, to increase the number of the "reserve army of labour"—that is, to increase the precariousness of life among the workers and to intensify the labour of those who serve the machines (as slaves their masters).[66]

Once compulsion to work was lifted, many of these machines, Morris believed, would no longer be necessary. Ultimately, it would be up to the community to decide which forms of technology best fostered rewarding lives for its members.

Morris's definition of socialism as a qualitative restructuring of work and society—a top-to-bottom reconceptualization of social relations, rather than simply a more equitable redistribution of existing work and goods—placed him in diametrical opposition to another utopian of his time, Edward Bellamy. Bellamy, whose proto–science fiction novel *Looking Backward* anticipates much of the postwork and luxury communism writing of today, envisioned a world of abundance and orderliness derived from the removal of the profit motive and reapportionment of the goods of existing society, which he believed would keep the productive base intact. In his review of the book, Morris recognized Bellamy's simplistic, undialectical belief that socialism could simply take what it pleased of modernity, totally intact, while getting rid of the bad parts. It represented a "half-change" that revealed Bellamy's perspective as rooted in "that of the industrious *professional* middle-class men of to-day purified from their crime of complicity with the monopolist class."[67]

Bellamy's utopia struck Morris the same way that bourgeois socialism struck Marx. In the *Manifesto*, Marx described the "more or less complete systems" worked out by middle-class reformist socialism as a fallacious half-change that neglected the necessity of struggle: "The Socialistic bourgeois want all the advantages of modern social conditions without the struggles and dangers necessarily resulting therefrom. They desire the existing state of society, minus its revolutionary and disintegrating elements. They wish for a bourgeoisie without a proletariat."[68]

In its worst versions, this bourgeois socialism insists that proletarians cease political struggle in favor of putting faith in economic growth and development: that "no mere political

reform, but only a change in the material conditions of existence, in economical relations, could be of any advantage to
them." Giving up on militant struggle to instead push for
political reforms would mean that this socialism would "in
no respect affect the relations between capital and labour,
but, at the best, lessen the cost, and simplify the administrative work, of bourgeois government."[69] Or, as Morris said of
Bellamy, "He conceives of the change to Socialism as taking
place without any breakdown of [modern] life, or indeed disturbance of it."[70]

Anyone who takes up the name of Marx to describe their
politics must take into account that Marxism is a theory of
struggle. The goal of Marx's critique of capitalism was not to
provide a set of instructions for managing the economy, but
to identify the contradictions and fissures, the places where
social struggle would be likely to emerge. Technology is an
important site of these struggles: not only is militant opposition to technology a historical fact, but it can suggest a more
liberatory politics of work and technology—one that is more
easily supported by Marx's work than are contemporary postwork utopias.

Instead of imagining a world without work that will
never come to pass, we should examine the ways historical
struggles posited an alternative relationship to work and liberation, where control over the labor process leads to greater
control over other social processes, and where the ends of
work are human enrichment rather than abstract productivity. Furthermore, these struggles point toward the only vehicle
for a liberation from capitalism: the composition of a militant
struggling class that attacks capital in all its manifold domina-
tions, including the technological.

In the next chapter, I turn toward technology's treatment on
the part of the twentieth-century organized workers' movement, including unions and labor parties. Their views largely
agreed with the postwork utopians: technology was politically

neutral, and could even be beneficial. Therefore, we must consult more heretical strains of Marxism among them—those who continued to question capitalist technology and valorize the anti-machine struggles of workers—if we are to provide an adequate postmortem of this disastrous strategic decision.

2

Tinkerers, Taylors, Soldiers, Wobs

On August 11, 1911, the molders at the Watertown Arsenal in Massachusetts, one of the United States' largest factories for military armaments, abruptly walked off the job. The action was spontaneous, unsanctioned by their union local, and was sparked by a simple piece of technology: the stopwatch.[1]

The dreaded "Taylor system" had come to Watertown. Under pressure to reduce costs, General William Crozier, the head of the Army's Ordinance Department, decided to adopt the latest techniques of "scientific management" developed by Frederick W. Taylor, a dyspeptic and fanatical engineer renowned among business leaders for improving industrial productivity.[2] Taylor and his team promised to rationalize manufacture, rendering it more efficient and productive, by determining the "one best way" for every aspect of the work process. Workers should follow detailed instructions on which tools to use, how fast to use them, how far to walk to various stations, and even what postures to adopt. But before those commands could be developed, the Taylorites had to study the labor process in depth. This is where the infamous stopwatch came in: the scientific managers timed each worker's every movement, breaking down work into a set of discrete tasks. Then they demanded workers speed them up.

As biographer Robert Kanigel describes it:

Formerly, the workmen earned a fixed amount for turning each tire to size. But once Taylor was through, their job was no longer to machine a tire but was a succession of smaller tasks: Set tire on machine ready to turn. Rough-face front edge. Finish-face front edge. Rough-bore front. And so on, each step minutely described and timed to the tenth of a minute.[3]

When one molder refused to be timed, he was summarily fired. His coworkers, already pushed to the edge by a week of scientific management, struck in solidarity. It was the beginning of a conflict that would eventually reach the halls of the US Congress.

Taylor was no stranger to facing workers' pitched resistance to his methods. In fact, he practically welcomed their hatred. The son of a wealthy Philadelphia lawyer, Taylor had prepared to attend Harvard and follow in his father's footsteps into the legal profession. But his nervous disposition caused him to abandon these plans, and instead he apprenticed to a machinist, working his way up into supervisory positions on the shop floor.

Taylor's factory career did not bestow upon him any special working-class consciousness; if anything, it only sharpened his contempt for workers, whom he viewed as stupid and lazy. His bête noire, going back to his experience as a foreman, was "soldiering," where workers toiled below their maximum effort. Taylor, with his factory floor experience, understood that workers could control their pace of work because they possessed a distinct advantage over their managers: their knowledge of the production process. At the turn of the century, it was the workers, rather than their overseers, who understood how manufacturing worked, and their methods for completing tasks were often based on intuitive and informal "rules of thumb": what color a chemical admixture should take, the appropriate heft of a specific part, and the like. Factory owners and managers might have only a dim idea about how products were actually put together, and no ability to do it themselves. This control of knowledge meant that workers could control the pace of work. Out of desire or necessity, they could slow it down, even stop it altogether.

Scientific management, for all its pretensions, was less about determining ideal working methods and more about shattering this tremendous source of worker power. By breaking apart each work process into carefully scrutinized component tasks, Taylor had cracked the secret of labor's advantage, thereby giving management complete mastery over the productive process. The modernizing terminology of "science" and "efficiency" masked the prerogatives of discipline and control of workers. In political economist Harry Braverman's estimation, "Taylor raised control to an entirely new plane when he asserted as an absolute necessity of adequate management the dictation to the worker of the precise manner in which work is to be performed."[4]

Taylor's own methods fell short of those of science. To get workers to obey his instructions, Taylor pulled from a mixed bag of deception, cajoling, and outright punishment. The best times achieved by the hardest workers became the new benchmarks for all workers; failure to measure up could mean docked pay. Often his "scientific" estimations of work rates were according to arbitrary metrics of his own invention. Reynold Spaeth, a physiologist who was a contemporary of Taylor's, noted that the latter's "law of heavy laboring," which stated that workers could handle heavy loads 43 percent of the day, lacked "all but the most fragmentary published data" and so must be accepted "on faith."[5] Most historians agree that the famous story of Schmidt, the "high-priced man" who quadrupled his rate of loading pig iron under Taylor's supervision, was a fabrication Taylor rarely tired of telling.[6]

Scientific management was, then, less a science of efficiency and more a political program for reshaping the worker as a pliant subject—what Taylor himself called "a complete mental revolution on the part of the workingmen ... toward their work, toward their fellow men, and toward their employers."[7]

This revolution had its own philosophy. According to historian Bryan Palmer, it was rooted in "a conservative analysis of men and human nature": that human beings were inherently lazy, that labor was machine-like, and that people's aspirations could ultimately be boiled down to acquisition of goods.[8] This "mental revolution" would be one of complete obedience.

Adam Smith had fretted, in *The Wealth of Nations*, that the division of labor could have a deleterious effect on the mind of the worker. Set to a repetitive task, "he naturally loses, therefore, the habit of such exertion, and generally becomes as stupid and ignorant as it is possible for a human creature to become."[9] For Taylor, what Smith referred to as the worker's "torpor of mind" was both his starting point and his end goal. "Now one of the very first requirements for a man who is fit to handle pig iron as a regular occupation is that he shall be so stupid and so phlegmatic that he more nearly resembles in his mental make-up the ox than any other type," Taylor wrote.[10] He never tired of likening workers to animals—horses, oxen, even songbirds and sparrows—in need of training and discipline.[11]

Unfortunately for Taylor, workers were rarely as easily controlled as a draft horse. At Bethlehem Steel in Pennsylvania, where he first began his experiments, a rash of mechanical breakdowns followed the imposition of Taylor's new time standards. The workers blamed the destruction on the elevated pace, but Taylor argued that "these men were deliberately breaking their machines as a part of the piece-work war which was going on" and forced workers to pay to repair machines.[12]

As Taylor's methods spread, so too did opposition. The strike at Watertown led to involvement from the union, which contacted friendly politicians in the area. In January 1912, Taylor and his men were called to account before Congress. There, Taylor's skittish and arrogant manner did little to advance his cause, especially when placed beside the testimony of workers, many of whom had worked at the arsenal for years. "It is humiliating to us, who have always tried to give to the Government the best that was in us," explained one of the molders. "This method is un-American in principle, and we most respectfully request that you have it discontinued at once."¹³ The unions supported this position. In a follow-up study, economist R.F. Hoxie catalogued "more than a hundred specific reasons" given by union representatives for fighting against the hated Taylor system. "Scientific management," he wrote, "properly applied, normally functioning, should it become universal, would spell the doom of effective unionism as it exists today."¹⁴

Remarkably, Congress took the side of the loyal arsenal workers and their union. Taylorism was discontinued at Watertown, and the fired molder was reinstated. Taylor was bewildered by the experience. As Hugh Aitken, historian of the Watertown strike, described it, Taylor was convinced the new method

> would do far more for the workers—if only they would "cooperate"—than unions ever had done or could do, for scientific management was based on an understanding of the laws of production, not upon the opinion of the ignorant. These laws could not be bargained over.¹⁵

Taylor himself never recovered from the grueling interrogations, and died in 1915. But his revolution was carried on, often by unlikely disciples: the leaders of radical workers' movements.

Leaders of the Marxist workers' movements of the early twentieth century viewed capitalist technologies like scientific management much as Taylor did: as an objective way to improve productivity, and therefore the condition of workers. Based on a particular interpretation of Marx's theory, they believed that capitalism, in its pursuit of profit, raised productivity through competitive technological innovation and the discovery of efficient working methods. These discoveries had no politics of their own; technology was neutral and could be appropriated with a change in ownership from private capital to state control, and thereby used to emancipate workers from drudgery. True, these new forms of work were difficult, dangerous, and widely hated. But if workers could table their protests about the productive forces, they could enjoy a world of plentiful goods and leisure—eventually. In other words, for orthodox Marxist theory, socialist production was *already contained* within the capitalist mode of production, as long as the capitalist mode of production could continue to develop.

This view of the objectivity and inevitability of technology, science, and progress in general was at the heart of the philosophies driving the most successful Marxist movements in history. Yet it was often at odds with the practical activity of workers themselves. Further, it shaped socialist strategy in ways ultimately detrimental to the goal of building emancipatory societies. These mistakes are not simply historical curios, but continue to influence left politics of technology. And so, before we can invent our future, we should return to the past and take stock of these movements' approaches to machines and technology.

The Second International

The struggles against mechanization in the nineteenth century detailed in the previous chapter were largely forgotten or suppressed by the official workers' movement as it grew in Europe in the first decades of the twentieth. Karl Kautsky, the so-called Pope of Marxism, had inherited Marx and Engels's legacy directly from Engels himself. As leading theoretician of the openly Marxist German Social Democratic Party (SPD), the nation's most popular political party, Kautsky exercised tremendous influence over the reception and interpretation of Marx's work, as well as the strategy of the workers' movement, coordinated through the congresses of the Second International. While many people's first encounter with Kautsky is through Lenin's polemical denunciations of him, Kautsky had enormous stature among Marxists, including Lenin himself, before the onset of the First World War.

Kautsky's "orthodox Marxism" portrayed socialism as a kind of destiny that would inevitably emerge from the husk of capitalism in accordance with scientific laws of history, driven by the motor of productive forces. As he put it: "In the last analysis, the history of mankind is determined, not by ideas, but by an economic development which progresses irresistibly, obedient to certain underlying laws and not to anyone's wishes or whims," bringing about "new forms of production which require new forms of society."[16] Socialism would arise on the basis of the development of capitalist production, which followed its own logic and laws.

In Kautsky's theory, the problem of capitalism was "the growing contradictions between the powers of production and the existing system of property," the solution to which could only be provided by socialism. He disavowed the most mechanical notions of transition:

> When we declare the abolition of private property in the means
> of production to be unavoidable, we do not mean that some fine
> morning the exploited classes will find that, without their help,
> some good fairy has brought about the revolution.

And yet, the Erfurt Program, the SPD manifesto coauthored by Kautsky, is full of fatalism: all capitalist development moves society closer to socialism, and any resistance to this, such as machine breaking, can only impede the revolution.

> The capitalist social system has run its course; its dissolution
> is now only a question of time. Irresistible economic forces
> lead with the certainty of doom to the shipwreck of capitalist

production. The substitution of a new social order for the existing one is no longer simply desirable, it has become inevitable.

This faith that the progression of capitalist production would
lead to a socialist destiny matched the SPD's cautious and
patient attitude toward building the power of the working
class through parliamentary means, with the party as its
vehicle. As the capitalist economy grew larger, more complex,
and more bureaucratic, it would thus require a political organ
to match. This meant the SPD tended to disdain demands for
workplace democracy. As Geoff Eley describes it in his history
of the European left, "Leading theorists like Karl Kautsky
specifically rejected workers' control, arguing that the com-
plexities of the advanced industrial economy and the modern
enterprise precluded bringing democratic procedures directly
into the economy itself."[17] Questions over the organization
of production were scientific, not political, affairs. Instead,
the SPD maintained, politics should train its sights on seizing
the reins of the economy by contesting for leadership of the
national parliament.

Yet, at the end of the nineteenth century, the inevitability
of socialism had come into doubt. While capitalist economies
had gone through a long period of decline, they seemed to
emerge, through consolidation into monopolies and trusts, into
a new phase of stability. As socialists scrambled to make sense
of the new situation, two leading perspectives emerged. One
pole, represented by Kautsky and the young Polish-German
communist Rosa Luxemburg, thought that the increased concentration of capital was the last step before a crisis and a
revolutionary situation. On the other, Erfurt Program coauthor
Eduard Bernstein argued that this indicated, rather, an unfore-
told resilience of capitalism, which meant that revolution was
off the table. Luxemburg's 1899 polemic against Bernstein's
"revisionism," *Social Reform or Revolution*, takes up this very
question. In it, she argues that the contradictions of capitalism

had not been overcome, but had been intensified, even as the final crisis was temporarily postponed. In doing so, Luxemburg reveals her continued debt to Kautskyian determinism: she counters Bernstein's "ethical socialism" with the "objective necessity of socialism, the explanation of socialism as the result of the material development of society"—in other words, a socialism proceeding mechanically from a terminal crisis stemming from internal contradictions of capitalist production.[18]

How did these heirs of "scientific socialism" differ in their approach from Marx himself? Lucio Colletti, in his philosophical analysis of Second International Marxism, points out that "the Marxism of that period transformed what Marx himself has declared a *historical tendency*"—that is, crisis—"into an 'inevitable law of nature.'"[19] Regardless of the differing views on breakdown and revolution, Bernstein, Kautsky, Luxemburg, and even figures outside of Germany such as Russian theorist Georgi Plekhanov all shared certain assumptions:

> The so-called "economic sphere"—which in Marx had embraced both the production of *things* and the production (objectification) of *ideas*; production and intersubjective communication; material production and the production of social relations (for Marx, the relation between man and nature was also a relationship between man and man, and vice versa)—was now seen as *one isolated factor*, separated from the other "moments" and thereby emptied of any effective *socio-historical* content, representing, on the contrary, an antecedent sphere, prior to any human mediation.[20]

In other words, the theory of the Second International had erred by constructing reified categories of an "economic base" of machines and a "superstructure" of language, law, and other elements of human sociality, which were merely epiphenomena of the base. By conceiving of the "economic base" as exclusively technologies—"production techniques"—and treating them as objective, "scientific" features of production, the Second International left out the social content of this production: the way production intimately shaped the arrangement of human beings, their culture, and their struggles. It was a socialist theory for which the content of class struggle was secondary, and for which capitalism's endogenous contradictions drove history and laid the groundwork for the transition to socialism.[21]

This determinist belief ultimately formed the basis of Kautsky's critique of the 1917 Bolshevik Revolution, which, in organizing a seizure of power in a peasant-majority country where capitalist social relations had only begun to take hold, had not followed the orderly progress of developmental stages. "It is an old Marxist saying," he admonished, "that revolutions cannot be made, but arise out of conditions."[22] This perspective informed Kautsky's Social Democratic Party's support for Germany, rather than a commitment to internationalism, during the onset of the First World War. As Eley describes it, the SPD's justification for betraying their internationalist commitments and supporting the war consisted, in part, of the argument that they were defending their gains against "tsarist reaction and Slavic backwardness," lending a "progressive" élan to a sudden lapse into nationalist militarism.[23]

After the war, Kautsky continued to adhere to what biographer Dick Geary terms his "mechanistic view of processes of historical change,"[24] arguing that socialism could only come about when the productive forces were sufficiently "ripe" (a term he repeatedly deployed). "Socialism cannot arise from a crippled and stagnant capitalism, but only from a capitalism carried to its highest point of productivity," he wrote in 1924. An entire Marxist tradition of endlessly deferred action and disdain for the struggles in the "periphery" of capitalist production has followed in its wake. To take one recent example, Bhaskar Sunkara, editor of *Jacobin* magazine, reiterates Kautskyian arguments about Marx in his recent *Socialist*

Manifesto: "The Third World's experience with socialism vindicates Marx," who "argued that a successful socialist economy requires already developed productive forces."[25]

Wobblies and the Technocrats

In the United States, which lacked the developed workers' parties of Europe, an alternate perspective prevailed. The Industrial Workers of the World (IWW), a massive organization of militant and transient workers and unemployed people that tended to prioritize direct action over all else, recognized the implications of scientific management for class struggle. As Taylorist "rationalization" spread through industry, the so-called Wobblies, as Mike Davis tells it, "attempted to develop a rank-and-file rebellion against the rationality of Taylor and the speed-up."[26] Amid a heightened interest among workers in militant opposition to the new work methods, the IWW published two remarkable tracts in 1913 on the topic of sabotage. After one of these pamphlets was used to prosecute an organizer, the union withdrew them from publication and publicly renounced sabotage as a tactic.

"Sabotage" at this time could mean any number of subversive techniques employed by a worker that interfered with production, including absenteeism, work slowdowns, "working to rule" by following only explicit requirements of the job, even striking. It could refer to disrupting equipment— "the displacement of parts of machinery or the disarrangement of a whole machine"—but it could also mean creating better-quality products than owners intended. As leading IWW member Walker C. Smith wrote,

> The workers are coming to see that their class is the one to
> whom adulterated food, shoddy clothing and rotten materials
> are sold, and by refusing to adulterate products they not only

41

destroy the employers' profits but safeguard their own lives as well.[27]

In fact, he argued with a note of irony, "sabotage" could even describe the actions of employers when they halted production by locking out workers.

Smith argued that the benefits of sabotage were twofold. First, it had a direct economic impact on capitalists: "The aim is to hit the employer in his vital spot, his heart and soul, in other words, his pocketbook." Second, and more important, it was a means of developing militancy and solidarity among workers. Smith likened its effects on class struggle to those of guerilla warfare:

> Guerilla warfare brings out the courage of individuals, it develops initiative, daring, resoluteness and audacity. Sabotage does the same for its users. It is to the social war what guerillas are to national wars. If it does no more than awaken a portion of the workers from their lethargy it will have been justified. But it will do more than that it will keep the workers awake and will incite them to do battle with masters. It will give added hope to the militant minority, the few who always bear the brunt of the struggle.

Sabotage techniques drew from the specific placement of workers within a production process, "a weapon which the masters cannot wrest from them." And if, like guerilla warfare, it was a weapon of the weak, then Smith admitted as much:

> Is it not true that the workers are still largely without consciousness of power? It would be suicidal to act on the theory that we are today clothed with the might for which we are struggling. Being weak we must guard our embryonic organization, using every means within our grasp save that of compromise with our enemy, the employing class.[28]

Legendary IWW activist Elizabeth Gurley Flynn attempted a more precise definition in her tract: "sabotage" referred to any effort "to limit his production in proportion to his remuneration," or in other words, "the deliberate withdrawal of efficiency by a competent worker." Rather than argue, as Smith did, for the salutary effects of sabotage for class consciousness, Flynn argued that workers *already* engaged in sabotage all the time, but without having a consistent name for what they were doing. Flynn quotes a worker at the Paterson silk mill in New Jersey, where organizers debated the efficacy of sabotage during the 1913 strike:

> I never heard of this thing called sabotage before Mr. Boyd spoke about it on the platform. I know once in a while when I want a half-day off and they won't give it to me I slip the belt off the machine so it won't run and I get my half day. I don't know whether you call that sabotage, but that's what I do.[29]

As Flynn noted, "one member of the executive committee after another admitted they had used this thing but they 'didn't know that was what you called it!'" Flynn's analysis of sabotage was, in this sense, eminently Marxist: rather than dictate strategy in a top-down manner, she conceptualized the actually existing tactics of workers as a fundamental component of class struggle. "We are to see what the workers are doing," she wrote, "and then try to understand why they do it; not tell them it's right or it's wrong, but analyze the condition."

A few years later, the themes and ideas from these infamous Wobbly tracts appeared in a somewhat surprising place: one of the major works of the unorthodox American sociologist Thorstein Veblen. Veblen's *The Engineers and the Price System* is most famous for his sketch of a technocratic socialist transformation in the United States. But the book opens with a somewhat odd discursus on, of all things, sabotage. Veblen reiterates the arguments of Smith and Flynn to such a degree that he must have had their work in mind. He even uses Flynn's definition of sabotage: "the conscientious withdrawal of efficiency."

Like the Wobblies, Veblen expanded the definition of sabotage to include techniques used by manufacturers in the course of business:

> Such manoeuvres of restriction, delay, and hindrance have a large share in the ordinary conduct of business; but it is only lately that this ordinary line of business strategy has come to be recognized as being substantially of the same nature as the ordinary tactics of the syndicalists.[30]

Many scholars have viewed Veblen's analysis as part of his characteristic ironic approach to criticizing the capitalists of his day, and such a tone is clearly evident.[31] But Veblen's discussion of sabotage also reflects his engagement with the IWW and their politics, which lasted for years. As economic historian John F. Henry describes, Veblen had a great deal of sympathy for the IWW, signing petitions against their persecution and going so far as to recommend that the American Farm Bureau hire out-of-work Wobblies to work the fields.[32] The latter suggestion prematurely ended his career at the Department of Agriculture.[33]

While Veblen likely shared the IWW's antipathy to capitalism, he did not approve of their methods. In describing the epidemic of sabotage committed by both workers and owners, he sought not to valorize the side of the workers, but to posit a mediating figure: the engineer. Veblen argued that engineers, whom he classified with the "common men" of the workforce rather than the "vested interests" of the capitalists, had "begun to become uneasily 'class conscious'" due to "a growing sense of waste and confusion in the management of industry by the financial agents of the absentee owners."[34] With their "common interest in productive efficiency, economical use of resources, and an equitable distribution of the consumable output" rather than profit and competition, engineers would be the worthy inheritors of the United States' industrial capacity, which they could run for the common good. They would form a "soviet of engineers."

Veblen died before he could do much more work on this front, but he inspired others to carry the torch of creating a more egalitarian society out of new technologies and restructured labor processes. One of the most influential and long-lasting think tanks dedicated to a society rationally administered by technical experts was organized by Howard Scott, a fast-talking engineer who had occasionally collaborated with Veblen.

In the 1920s, Scott had been the research director of the IWW, studying waste in the capitalist system; in 1932, with engineering professor Walter Rautenstrauch, he formed the Committee on Technocracy at Columbia University.[35] Like Veblen, the Technocrats criticized the "price system" they saw as the root problem with capitalism, arguing instead for a currency system based on "energy units," a plan that was never fully explained. Even amid these somewhat crankish schemes, Technocracy reached the zenith of its influence in the early 1930s as the Great Depression shattered faith in the existing economic system and sent people looking for answers to what would come next.

Technocracy's diagnosis of the capitalist system sounds remarkably like the predictions of today's Fully Automated radicals: that a social crisis was upon us, caused by the substitution of machines for laborers. As the Technocrats avowed in their eponymous magazine, from ditch digging to adding machines,

one machine after another has been or is being perfected to take the place of the worker. It is, however, obvious that it is only a question of time when machines will have displaced so many

45

workers that an entirely new system of providing the people of
the earth with a living must be devised.[36]

What would this system look like? By deploying machinery
to reduce labor hours, and by eliminating methods of wealth
accumulation through money, the Technocrats maintained that
"if every man labored a little more than six hundred hours
a year for twenty years, his efforts would entitle him to an
income of approximately $20,000 a year!"[37] In today's dollars,
such a universal basic income would place a household in the
top 1 percent of earners. But it was the embrace of the machine
that was the raison d'être of Technocracy: "Why should we
fight machinery when under the system of Technocracy we
could make machines do more and more of our work so that
we would have more and more leisure to enjoy life?"[38]

The vogue for Technocracy proved short lived: a "media
fad and political dead end" in the estimation of engineering historian David F. Noble, and one that took increasingly
cultish turns.[39] Indeed, Scott's organization, Technocracy, Inc.,
still exists today, decades after his death, and its rudimentary
website promotes postwork futures and environmentalism-
oriented experiments like aquaponics. Ultimately, for all its
lofty (and occasionally bizarre) goals, the organization was
content to merely outline the problem and hypothetical solutions. During the Depression, the IWW, weakened after years
of repression, showed some initial interest in Technocracy. For
instance, one *Industrial Worker* headline from 1933 screamed,
"Scientist Predicts End of Capitalism within Three Years,"
though Scott, the "scientist" in question, had exaggerated
his credentials. However, the IWW eventually tired of these
visions and subjected Technocracy to a pithy critique: "Aside
from their columns of figures and determinations, they do not
have a program for accomplishing things, and they completely
exclude the class struggle, so there is nothing left to discuss
there."[40]

Lenin and the Bolsheviks

The Bolsheviks shared much of the theoretical outlook of Second International, despite differences in political strategy. Even after the Russian Revolution, building socialism in the "backward" Soviet Union was largely a matter of acquiring capitalist technologies in order to speed through the stages of development thought necessary for a socialist economy. One historian remarks that a faith in science prevailed among all classes and political tendencies in Russia, including the Bolsheviks, part of a longer discourse about the empire's need to "catch up" to the level of Britain, France, and Germany.[41]

In spite of a general acceptance of a stagist road to socialism, there was much debate among Bolshevik intellectuals over the question of technology and the labor process. On the philosophical plane, Nikolai Bukharin took a technologically determinist position similar to Kautsky's, sketching a linear notion of development via the economic "base," with technology as an autonomous actor. He writes, "The historic mode of production, i.e. the form of society, is determined by the development of the productive forces, i.e. the development of technology."[42]

Philosopher Georg Lukács criticized this view, noting the alignment between Bukharin's analysis and the ideology of the capitalist world's view of science: "The closeness of Bukharin's theory to bourgeois, natural-scientific materialism derives from his use of 'science' (in the French sense) as a model." Lukács insisted that a true historical materialist analysis meant that science and technology could not be divorced from the class system in which they were embedded. "In its concrete application to society and history," he wrote, "it therefore frequently obscures the specific feature of Marxism: *that all economic or 'sociological' phenomena derive from the social relations of men to one another*."[43] For Lukács, this meant that capitalist production is not so easily divorced from capitalism's class

47

structure and its prerogatives to rule and control workers, particularly at the point of production.

Lenin himself often appeared to lean toward Bukharin's side, believing that technology was independent of social relations, and that the Soviet Union needed to adopt capitalist production methods. In his writing on the "Taylor system," Lenin theorized that while Taylorism was a form of enslavement under capitalism, under socialism it would alleviate the burdens of labor:

> The Taylor system—without its initiators knowing or wishing it—is preparing the time when the proletariat will take over all social production and appoint its own workers' committees for the purpose of properly distributing and rationalising all social labour. Large-scale production, machinery, railways, telephone —all provide thousands of opportunities to cut by three-fourths the working time of the organised workers and make them four times better off than they are today.[44]

In essence, the efficiency gains produced by Taylorized production, which simply meant a greater intensity of exploitation under capitalism, could be realized under socialist ownership of the means of production as the reduction of work hours— eventually, once adequate development had been achieved. Elsewhere, Lenin expressed a more ambivalent attitude, referring to Taylorism as "a combination of the refined brutality of bourgeois exploitation and a number of the greatest scientific achievements."[45] Eager to raise productivity in the fledgling Soviet Union, he ultimately argued for "combining the Soviet power and the Soviet organisation of administration with the up-to-date achievements of capitalism" such as Taylorism.[46]

The subject of Taylorism sparked much debate among the Bolsheviks. Alexander Bogdanov, whose Proletkult initiatives sought to construct a worker-oriented culture and aesthetics as an alternative to bourgeois artistic forms, criticized the adoption of Taylorist methods. Bogdanov believed that Taylorism would undermine the goals of the revolution by forcing workers into repetitive tasks that would cause their critical and creative abilities to atrophy. Instead, Bogdanov believed that socialist production would be characterized by "a highly developed mental equality of the workers as universally developed conscious producers."[47] Furthermore, he recognized that Taylorism relied upon a strict managerial control, which could introduce divisions among workers, especially between laborers and engineers.[48]

On the other side of the debate was Alexei Gastev, a former poet who became the head of the Central Institute of Labor. For Gastev, Taylorism's chief partisan among the Bolsheviks, scientific management was not simply a matter of efficiency, but a means for the creation of a new socialist subject and a modernist utopia. As Richard Stites describes it in his cultural history of the Soviet Union, Gastev envisioned "a mechanized, standardized world, in a literal sense, with production ruled by self-regulating and self-correcting machines, joined throughout the world in a machine city—that is, a single unbroken mechanized civilization stretching around the globe." Gastev was emphatic: machines should set the pace not only of work, but of all social life, which would hence become rationalized and standardized—"a single mode of speech, a standardized catalog of thoughts, and a unified collection of meals, of housing, and of sexual and spiritual life."[49]

Such rationalization effaced any need for democracy, as society would be more like a machine in need of tinkering than an unruly assemblage of individuals and groups. These outdated political forms should be banished, he reasoned, along with outdated production methods:

> The method of solving social problems by "vote" and by finding the majority or minority must be seen as old-fashioned hand production; the essence of the new industry will be to end this and to create new means of revealing the general will.[50]

Indeed, a machinic class of workers could mean a machinic governance: "Machines from being managed will become managers."[51]

Gastev was forced to moderate his wildest flights of techno-utopian fancy in the face of pushback from workers and other members of the intelligentsia, who wanted room for the human being within the production process. But, due to intense pressure to rapidly boost productivity, the Soviet Taylorists ultimately won out, and massive state-driven industrialization and bureaucratic management became the means to create a new socialist subject. While policy was articulated in the ambivalent language of Lenin—Taylorism was, in the last analysis, a means to alleviate the burdens of workers—workers experienced it more as Taylor himself had described it: as a means to enforce labor discipline at the expense of the autonomy of workers. Those workers, who had fought and sacrificed for proletarian democracy, responded with bitter opposition to the machinic organization of labor. According to Paul Avrich, a historian of anarchism, the rebellious workers and sailors of Kronstadt identified "the Taylor system" as one of their grievances against the Bolshevik government.[52]

By the time of the Great Purge of the 1930s, Gastev and many of the other Taylorist utopians were marginalized and executed under Stalin, though their preferred methods remained Soviet industrial policy. As Stites describes it, "Only the crudest and harshest elements of Taylorism were retained, but stripped of all dreamlike qualities and aspirations and made into tools of labor exploitation."[53] The massive manufacturing center at Magnitogorsk, built under Stalin's first Five-Year Plan, emblematized this prevailing theory of technology and socialism. While under Lenin, Soviet efficiency and productivity had weighed weakly against working conditions and proletariat politics, Stalin's program saw industrial development as simply *synonymous* with socialism.[54] Thus, even while class struggle was refracted away from the shop floor and toward competition with the capitalist world, it made no difference to Stalin that American engineers designed the Magnitogorsk complex, or that the great Soviet industrial city of was modeled on a city located in the heart of American capitalist production: Gary, Indiana.[55] The Marxist philosopher Louis Althusser suggests that this represents a weakness Stalin shared with Kautsky and the German Social Democratic Party: "Might it not be that Stalin fell short of Lenin's politics, as his 1938 text attests, veering towards the tradition of the Second International's politics, the politics of the primacy of the productive forces over the relations of production?"[56]

For their part, Soviet workers repeatedly resisted and rebelled at the point of production. During the construction of Magnitogorsk, laborers revolted over the difficult conditions, sabotaging the construction or simply running away.[57] Jeffrey Rossman documents that during the first Five-Year Plan, resistance by textile workers

included mass demonstrations, bread riots, strikes, slowdowns, industrial sabotage, subversive speeches at factory assemblies, acts of violence against local authorities, written protests to party leaders, anonymous leafleting, and the composition and circulation of subversive works of the imagination (chiefly, songs and poems).[58]

These workers rebelled on the grounds that the ideals of the Bolshevik Revolution, which included limits to toil and baseline compensation, were being undermined by Stakhanovite ideology celebrating total devotion to work.[59] Thus, alterations to the labor process, characterized by the loss of control and intensifications of Taylorism, were a chief flashpoint of labor strife. And, similar to their forbears of a century before, this strife manifested in breaking the new machines.

Sabotage had a number of advantages for the Soviet worker. For one, it directly expressed an opposition to new labor processes centered around new industrial equipment, and it did so in a less public way than strikes or demonstrations, which could lead to punishment. And even when resistance took more overt forms such as work stoppages, sabotage was an important component, as it became a means to enforce discipline among the entire labor force. Would-be strikebreakers often found their machines incapacitated, and when shock-work brigades and labor competitions among young workers threatened the overall pace of work, they too found their equipment destroyed. "In Teikovo, Vichuga, and Iaroslavl," Rossman notes, "unidentified 'class enemies'—veteran operatives, no doubt—sabotaged the looms of those taking part in the Competition for Best Weaver and Overlooker."[60]

Walter Benjamin's Dissent

Across his essays and philosophical writings, Walter Benjamin remained a perennial critic of the notion of progress rife in the Marxism of his day. In his *Arcades Project*, for instance, Benjamin sought "to demonstrate a historical materialism which has annihilated within itself the idea of progress."[61] Yet Benjamin was neither a primitivist nor a romantic. Particularly when it came to new technologies of media and cultural production, Benjamin was optimistic, and in his famous essay "The Work of Art in the Age of Mechanical Reproduction," he marveled at the ability of photography and film to abolish the distance between the masses and art, and to reveal the contingency of everyday life:

> By close-ups of the things around us, by focusing on hidden details of familiar objects, by exploring commonplace milieus under the ingenious guidance of the camera, the film, on the one hand, extends our comprehension of the necessities which rule our lives; on the other hand, it manages to assure us of an immense and unexpected field of action.[62]

Similarly, the spread of publishing techniques meant that "the distinction between author and public" was "about to lose its basic character."[63] Moreover, Benjamin argued that the presumption of bourgeois "competence" tied to cultural work should be broken down by new technologies, and that more workers should be brought into the sphere of intellectual production.[64]

These views horrified Benjamin's interlocutor Theodor Adorno, who wrote extensively on the degradation of cultural production, specifically music, via technologies of reproduction. But more important than Adorno's oft-cited technological antipathy, musicians themselves fought against recordings, which they recognized as rendering them superfluous. In San Francisco, theaters were repeatedly hit with stench bombs for refusing to hire orchestras; in St. Louis, unionized musicians planted time bombs that damaged the Vitaphone sound film equipment that had replaced them.[65]

As fascism, itself an ideological formation imbued with an infatuation with machines, continued to march victoriously through Europe, Benjamin sought to evaluate the historic failure of German socialism. Writing in 1940, shortly before his death, he located its essential mistake in the belief in progress connected to the further development of productive technologies:

> There is nothing which has corrupted the German working-class so much as the opinion that *they* were swimming with the tide. Technical developments counted to them as the course of the stream, which they thought they were swimming in. From this, it was only a step to the illusion that the factory-labor set forth by the path of technological progress represented a political achievement.[66]

As Michael Löwy describes it in his study of the text, Benjamin attacks "the essential article of faith" of the Second

International's strategy: that victory for socialism amounted to a rapidly expanding balance sheet, "the quantitative accumulation of productive forces, of the gains of the labour movement, of the number of party members and voters in a movement of linear, irresistible, 'automatic' progress."[67]

Historian Mary Nolan sketches a portrait of interwar Germany that supports Benjamin's dialectical inversions. Evolutionary beliefs, she notes, continued to characterize large portions of the fragmented German left into the Weimar years: "The [SPD]'s unifying theory was an updated version of Kautskyian orthodoxy, provided by Rudolf Hilferding, and displayed all the economic determinism and political passivity of the original."[68] And even while the German Communist Party (KPD) criticized the techniques of Fordism and Taylorism as increasing exploitation, "the Communists were equally convinced that the same technology that served capitalism could also serve socialism."[69] Ultimately, "the shared productivism and technological determinism of the Second and Third Internationals led to a shared inability to imagine any forms of production other than highly rationalized ones."[70]

Such rationalized work did not merely reproduce structures of domination on the shop floor; it was also deleterious to the health and well-being of the workers. Nolan notes that injuries and illnesses, particularly "nervous ailments," skyrocketed after rationalization.[71] And, as processes became more efficient, throwing people out of work, the socialist politicians who continued to back rationalization policies lost legitimacy among their members, leading to generalized resentment toward Weimar social democracy. While leaders hemmed and hawed about the effects of new technologies, workers were increasingly of one, hostile, voice.[72]

Rather than a natural outgrowth of history's progression, for Benjamin, a revolutionary class has to "explode the continuum of history." Indeed, this history is not a tale of progress, or even a succession of events, but "one single catastrophe, which unceasingly piles rubble on top of rubble and hurls it before his feet."[73] Elsewhere, Benjamin is even more explicit on this point: "Marx says that revolutions are the locomotive of world history. But perhaps it is quite otherwise. Perhaps revolutions are an attempt by the passengers on this train—namely, the human race—to activate the emergency brake."[74] Here an openly *decelerationist* Benjamin emerges. Technology does not lead toward a revolutionary break, nor does a revolution necessarily spur on new technological developments. Rather, Benjamin reconceives revolution as a cessation of catastrophe. It halts "progress" in its tracks.

What will motivate this revolutionary action, if not the faith in technological progress upon which the Second International wagered its fortunes? Benjamin looks to the past for inspiration, though not to see the wonders achieved by the bourgeoisie, as Marx and Engels did in the heady days of 1848. Instead, Benjamin looks to class struggle. While that struggle may be one of loss and catastrophe, it has bequeathed to the present "fine and spiritual" qualities:

> They are present as confidence, as courage, as humor, as cunning, as steadfastness in this struggle, and they reach far back into the mists of time. They will, ever and anon, call every victory which has ever been won by the rulers into question.[75]

Löwy clarifies:

> What interests [Benjamin] in the past is not the development of the productive forces, the contradiction between the forces and relations of production, forms of property or state forms or the development of modes of production—essential themes of Marx's work—but the life and death struggle between oppressors and oppressed, exploiters and exploited, dominators and dominated.[76]

Here Benjamin sounds similar notes as the Wobbly proponents of sabotage. Redemption from capitalism and its violence will not come from a simple appropriation of its devices. Instead, he suggests, it is borne on the backs of those sedimented experiences of the nameless people who fought against them, who broke, jammed, sabotaged—who grabbed for the emergency brake—in their circumstances. This is the raw material of future emancipation.

3

Against Automation

What is automation? As we have seen, machines have replicated and augmented human work processes for centuries, and that is often the colloquial use of "automation" in our current moment. But "automation" was not used to describe this process until 1947, when Delmar Harder, vice president of manufacturing at Ford Motor Company, created its Automation Department. The department's engineers redesigned automobile production so that materials were automatically conveyed from one process to another, obviating the need for laborers to load and unload machines.[1] Further, the process was itself increasingly machine-controlled, through a system of timers, switches, and relays—what technology historian David Hounsell calls the "electromechanical brain."[2]

Most of the technologies involved in automation had been developed and implemented in other industries years before their incorporation into Ford's production process. What made automation new was its centrality to Ford's manufacturing strategy, coming at a time of historic unrest among autoworkers, and in particular, on the heels of a costly twenty-four-day strike at Ford's massive River Rouge plant in May of 1949. Not only would the new technologies dramatically reduce an unruly labor force, but they allowed Ford to decentralize its production away from the roiling unrest of Detroit as the company opened new automated factories in Cleveland and Buffalo.[3] Workers immediately perceived the threat, and automation was, from its inception, a deeply politicized issue.

Today, the headlines scream about automation's potential to replace workers, often in language reminiscent of anti-immigrant rhetoric: robots are threatening to "take" or "steal" jobs. You can even go to the website willrobotstakemyjob.com and input specific occupations to get statistics on the likelihood of such theft. Writers have only a 3.8 percent chance—"totally safe"—while machinists face an alarming 65 percent. "Robots are watching," the site cautions. These numbers are drawn from a widely cited 2013 report by economist Carl Benedikt Frey and computer scientist Michael A. Osborne that concluded 47 percent of total US employment would be automated by 2034.[4]

Many writers on the radical left have accepted this framing of automation, and even extended and detourned its implications, making "full automation" central to the transcendence of capitalist exploitation. In *Inventing the Future*, Alex Williams and Nick Srnicek argue, "Without full automation, postcapitalist futures must necessarily choose between abundance at the expense of freedom (echoing the work-centricity of Soviet Russia) or freedom at the expense of abundance, represented by primitivist dystopias."[5] Peter Frase's *Four Futures*, which plays out an assortment of postcapitalisms, utopian and dystopian, holds "perfect automation" as "the constant in [the] equation."[6] And Aaron Bastani's *Fully Automated Luxury Communism* pushes this idea to its limits, promising a future of boundless leisure for all, supplemented by a profusion of goods and services delivered sans human exploitation: "We will see more of the world than ever before, eat varieties of food we never have heard of, and lead lives equivalent—if we so wish—to those of today's billionaires."[7]

Such a framing is both simple and attractive, especially to those of us trapped in dead-end jobs and eking out precarious existences; if robots, rather than if we and our fellow workers, performed these tasks, and the productivity of technology were widely dispersed, maybe we could live our lives like the rich do.

Like those cheesy banner ads that were all over the web in the late 2000s, you could have a fulfilling egalitarian society with "one weird trick." The bourgeoisie would hate this!

The problem for Full Automators, of any political leaning, is that their predictions rely on a faulty understanding of what actually happens when machines are introduced into production processes. In other words, "perfect automation" has little to do with actually existing automation. David Autor, an economist, offers a useful corrective to this mistake in his 2015 article "Why Are There Still So Many Jobs?," its plaintive title a response to John Maynard Keynes's rosy predictions of a future with a reduced work week. As Autor explains, rather than simply replace human jobs with machinic processes, automation affects labor in complex ways:

> Changes in technology do alter the types of jobs available and what those jobs pay. In the last few decades, one noticeable change has been "polarization" of the labor market, in which wage gains went disproportionately to those at the top and at the bottom of the income and skill distribution, not to those in the middle.[8]

Automation thus recomposes the workforce, isolating and rearranging tasks, altering job descriptions, and hollowing out middle-tier occupations.

Why does automation polarize instead of outright replace jobs? For one, many jobs require labor that is challenging to automate. Computers have to follow instructions laid out by programmers, so in order to substitute a computer for a worker, the worker's tasks must be understood and articulated. However, much of the labor process is encompassed in tacit knowledge that workers are unable to articulate: "There are tasks for which neither computer programmers nor anyone else can enunciate the explicit 'rules' or procedures."[9] Even when tasks are known, automating them is easier said than done. On one end, computers cannot replicate the high levels of abstract thought required for managerial positions. On the other, jobs that require both manual work and flexibility, such as service sector jobs in food preparation and maintenance, are both difficult and cost-prohibitive to automate.

Take an example. In March 2018, Flippy, a burger-flipping robot, was rolled out at the Pasadena location of fast-food chain CaliBurger, to great fanfare and numerous headlines. The implication was clear: Would this spell the end of fast-food jobs, the mascot for low-skilled entry-level occupations? Not exactly. In an event that provoked far less press coverage, Flippy was retired after one day of work. CaliBurger's owners took the honorable path of blaming Flippy's failure on their human employees: workers were simply too slow with tasks such as dressing the burgers, causing Flippy's achievements to pile up. However, a few discerning journalists had previously noted Flippy's numerous errors in the relatively simple task that gave the robot its name. And so, yet another fully automated dream came crashing into messy reality.[10]

According to Autor, the introduction of new kinds of information and control technology, such as what is currently hyped as "artificial intelligence," supplements managerial work, and so increases the power and wages of bosses. On the other end, manual laborers (such as Flippy's coworkers) see tasks eaten away and their movements reorganized and tightly controlled to make room for more rigid machines. Wages and working conditions deteriorate. But even then, automation stops short of "full": such systems, as we will see, rely upon a stratum of human labor that is all but ineradicable. This is as true of Flippy as it is of the most powerful AI.

What do tend to be substitutable are not the lowest rungs, but those jobs requiring repetitive physical labor, as well as middle management jobs in operations. For example, Amazon's warehouses use a software-directed system that coordinates human laborers, who select individual goods, with robots, who move large shelves. Algorithms replace middle-income jobs in managing the floor, leading to a polarized workforce of increasingly wealthy and powerful executives and increasingly degraded laborers who are substitutable not by machines, but by other humans; in other words, they are eminently replaceable.

Another way to put this is to use the language of Italian *operaismo* (workerism), which, half a century ago, tracked these movements very carefully as new technologies descended upon the vast and turbulent workforces of the Turin auto factories. Part of the phenomenon Autor describes as "polarization" was articulated in the workerist language of class struggle as "decomposition of the working class."[11] Reorganizing the labor process was a powerful way to disrupt how workers had organized themselves against the bosses. And wherever automation was implemented, it met pitched resistance backed by worker-led militant research, independent of official labor leadership.

In May of 1956, the British Parliament took up a discussion of an industrial dispute at the Standard Motor Company in Coventry. Workers had been on strike for over a week, angered by the company's announcement that 3,000 employees, rendered redundant by the adoption of new automation technologies, would be fired. Some members of Parliament put pointed questions to the Tory minister of labour, Iain Macleod: was he "aware that the introduction of automation in industry is giving rise to serious misgiving among the organised workers"? Macleod attempted to assuage these concerns with little more than platitudes, appealing to automation's contribution to "the prosperity and happiness of the nation" and blithely ignoring its imminent impact on jobs. "It is welcomed by the Government," he replied, "and responsible opinion on both sides of industry as essential to our future efficiency and, therefore, to the continuance of full employment."[12] In response, Labour MP William Owen struck a conciliatory note:

Is the Minister aware that organised workers are by no means limited to the philosophy of the Luddite movement these days but welcome the development of a new technique in modern industry? However, they are seriously concerned with the probable economic and social effect of the new machines unless there is—as the Minister has indicated—a real possibility of early consultation between both sides of industry, with Government co-operation.[13]

Owen portrayed the Coventry strikers as potentially willing to adopt new technology, provided their jobs were preserved, with the help of government policy. Such measures would not be forthcoming. Less than two months after an uneasy resolution of the Standard Motor Company strike, the British Motor Company announced immediate layoffs of 6,000 workers. Perhaps those workers subscribing to the philosophy of the Luddite movement were right after all.

Across the English Channel in France, Cornelius Castoriadis, a theorist and cofounder of the libertarian socialist group Socialisme ou Barbarie, observed these events closely. Two elements of these struggles stuck out to him. First, automation represented a new phase of class struggle, "a capital offensive against labor, considered as the originating force in production," with the eventual goal of "the elimination of man qua man from the sphere of production"—a goal Castoriadis believed was ultimately impossible, even while it exercised a decisive influence over the course of class struggle.[14] Second, he noted that the strikes emerged from the workers and their chosen representatives, the shop stewards, in contravention of the trade union leadership.

This latter factor—autonomous worker action against both management and union leadership—would mark the struggles against automation in the postwar era. While unions counseled caution and patience, workers paid them little heed, walking off jobsites and vandalizing machines. And on the vanguard of opposing automation were those often marginalized by the official workers' movement—women and African Americans—who produced some of the most enduring critical knowledge of new technologies.

Automation as Control

The fight against machines that Castoriadis noticed in Coventry had begun more than a decade earlier, as part of the dramatic restructuring of the industrial economy during World War II. Though the term did not achieve widespread use until after the war's cessation, automation's major victory began with the development of numerically controlled machine tools, which could replace the skilled machinists who had been required for heavy manufacturing. While automation's defenders, such as Macleod, pointed to the gains in "efficiency" brought by the new methods, David Noble's historical research on the process tells a different story. The introduction of automation occurred through the prerogatives of the war economy, what Dwight D. Eisenhower would later dub the "military-industrial complex." This meant that military values, not commercial ones, impacted the new forms of production:

First was the emphasis placed on performance rather than cost in order to meet the requirements of the military mission ... Then there was the insistence upon command, the precise specification, communication, and execution of orders, uncompromised by either intermediary error or judgment. Finally, there was the preoccupation with modern methods, high technology and capital-intensive, to guarantee performance and command objectives and thereby assure the success of the mission: national security against communism.[15]

In other words, the priority for production during the war was consistency and control, not saving time or increasing profits, though wartime demand and wage controls kept corporate coffers full. An alternative form of automation popular among machinists, "record-playback," was never seriously pursued, although it was also efficient. Unlike numeric control, the record-playback method was analog, storing the precise movement of a machinist, and so still required a skilled hand. Rather than pursue efficiency, management sought to wrest control of production away from the machinists.[16]

Military planners and industrialists urgently felt the need for total control during the war. The US workforce reached a pinnacle of unruliness in the 1940s, with the number of strikes per year surpassing the previous high-water mark reached during the Great Depression. On average, Ford plants experienced strike activity every other day. And these strikes were a form of double defiance: of wartime laws forbidding strikes, on one hand, and of pledges of unions to keep a lid on unrest, on the other. Moreover, a clear pattern emerged in which worker rebellion against automation was marked by wildcat strikes.[17]

The need for absolute control over machines permeated the sciences at the time, which themselves were coordinated by the military through the Office of Scientific Research and Development. One emerging branch of research promised to solve this puzzle across a variety of scientific and engineering disciplines by uncovering mechanisms that heralded a future of self-regulated machines: cybernetics. Derived from the Greek word for "steering," cybernetics sought to develop machines that could incorporate "feedback" reflexively into their operation. In other words, they eliminated the need for human control. Norbert Wiener, the mathematician who coined the term "cybernetics" and provided many of its early breakthroughs, began this work with research on the creation of Allied anti-aircraft weapons that were more effective at targeting a zigzagging enemy pilot. In this, as Peter Galison notes, cybernetics as a project centers on a specific problem: how to predict the behavior of a calculating, but opaque, opponent, or a "Manichean devil."[18] On the battlefield, this could mean a tank commander or a fighter pilot. In the context of the factory, these devils could be the workers themselves.

Wiener, whose political sympathies were to the left of many of his military-minded colleagues, realized the terrifying implications of his work. He ultimately abandoned military research after the nuclear attacks on Japan, turning toward social criticism of cybernetics through books and essays written for popular audiences. Beyond the specter of nuclear annihilation, Wiener was concerned with domestic uses of cybernetics: industrial automation. Wiener thought this would be a catastrophe for workers, writing that automation "gives the human race a new and most effective collection of mechanical slaves to perform its labor ... any labor that accepts the conditions of competition with slave labor, accepts the conditions of slave labor, and is essentially slave labor."[19]

Wiener did not believe that cybernetics would create a condition where an autonomous technology confronted increasingly superfluous human beings. Rather than a machines-versus-mankind, *Terminator*-style dystopia so popular in science fiction fantasies of artificial intelligence, he viewed the automatic machine as a potential weapon to be used by powerful people to control others: "Its real danger, however, is the quite different one that such machines, though helpless by themselves, may be used by a human being or a block of human beings to increase their control over the rest of the human race."[20] In other words, automation would be a weapon of class war.

Armed with this insight, Wiener wrote to Walter Reuther, head of the United Automobile Workers, detailing the plans of the industrialists who had attempted to hire Wiener to consult on automating their factories. Although Wiener had refused, he knew other researchers would happily take such positions. He wanted to give Reuther the opportunity to get in front of the "disastrous" levels of unemployment that would result. In his letter, Wiener proposed two alternatives for Reuther to explore. First, he could agitate to "secure the profits in [new machines] to an organization dedicated to the benefit of labor": an automation fund. But Wiener also held out the possibility that the technology itself was too dangerous.

> It may be on the other hand, that you think the complete suppresion [sic] of these ideas is in order. In either case, I am willing to back you loyally, and without any demand or request for personal returns in what I consider will be a matter of public policy.[21]

After intermittent correspondence, Reuther invited Wiener to speak at a UAW conference in 1952, but Wiener, suffering from depression-related illness, declined.

The JFT and the Miners

Instead of heeding Wiener's warnings, labor leaders would come to embrace the new machines, cajoled by an aggressive campaign launched by the business elite. Capitalists had been spooked by wartime militancy, which threatened to intensify as millions of soldiers returned to the labor market from overseas. They had flown into action, pushing through coercive initiatives like the 1947 Taft-Hartley Act, but had also held out a few carrots. Firms negotiated with major unions, such as the UAW and the United Mine Workers of America, to tie wage increases to increases in productivity. This meant that labor would accept whatever new machinery businesses introduced, thereby ceding control of the production process to management. So compliant was the union leadership that in 1950, *Fortune* called UMWA head John L. Lewis "the best salesman the machinery industry ever had."[22] Even lightly held reservations about new technology provoked opprobrium among progress- (and business-) minded commentators. As labor economist Ben Seligman complained, "Whenever an exasperated labor leader asserts that automation can be a curse, the head of the U.S. Chamber of Commerce responds that he is a Luddite."[23]

Yet this increased productivity derived, to a large extent, from speeding up the production process; "efficiencies" were borne by the workers' bodies and by the miseries of those thrown into unemployment. Discontent was on the rise. As resistance to automation erupted from below, it would be documented and theorized by Marxist groups, such as Socialisme ou Barbarie, who were estranged from major political parties and trade unions. These groups viewed their task as the analysis of actually existing class struggles at the point of production. Real socialism could follow only from this struggle, not from the endlessly deferred utopias of leisure and abundance imposed through negotiations between bureaucratic unions and capitalists.

In the United States, the Johnson-Forest Tendency, a group of worker-militants who splintered from the American Trotskyist movement, took a keen interest in the postwar transformations at the point of production and the clashes that ensued. With many members embedded in factories, the JFT understood that increased productivity was squeezed out of the small moments of downtime, bits of reprieve from work, to which workers had become accustomed. They produced a pamphlet, *The American Worker*, that described this transition in the auto plants: "The worker used to be able to smoke more often. Now he has to spend all day watching, changing and cleaning tools. The interludes are briefer. The end of the day produces a more exhausted worker, mentally and physically."[24]

As conditions deteriorated and the acquiescence of the union bureaucracy continued, workers wildcatted. And one set of wildcat strikes in particular captured the attention of the JFT's "Forest," the pseudonym of Raya Dunayevskaya, a writer and activist who was formerly Trotsky's personal secretary. For months in 1949 and 1950, miners walked off the job and shut down mines with roving pickets in response to the introduction of the continuous miner—or, in the words of the miners, the "man killer."[25] It was the first strike against automation, and in it, Dunayevskaya saw the seed of a new kind of radical politics.

The JFT's "Johnson," the nom de guerre of the great Trinidadian activist and writer C.L.R. James, did not share Dunayevskaya's perspective. In *Facing Reality*, cowritten with Grace Lee Boggs and Cornelius Castoriadis after a split with Dunayevskaya, James took a line that was uncharacteristically technologically determinist. The expulsion of workers from the production process indicated "a system committing suicide." For James, automation meant a potentially greater level of organization and control of production by workers:

> Production as a whole can only be controlled by the producers as a whole in their shop floor organizations. Thus, far more than in any other country, the automation of industry in the United States is creating the actual conditions for a Government of Workers Councils.[26]

Dunayevskaya viewed the struggle itself, pitched against both the mine owners and the collaborationist UMWA, as producing a new perspective on work as a whole among the miners:

> Instead of asking for high wages, the miners raised altogether new questions dealing with their *conditions* of work, and questions of the work itself. What they asked was: "What *kind* of labor should man do?" "Why should there be such a gulf between thinking and doing?"[27]

For Dunayevskaya, automation's reception divided along class lines, determined by one's relationship to the machine. While capitalists, management, and the union leadership praised automation as a progressive force, those who experienced it directly had a completely different view. "If you are the one who operates it," she wrote, "you feel its impact in every bone of your body: you are more sweaty, more tired, more tense and you feel about as useful as a fifth wheel."

Dunayevskaya mercilessly criticized the "labor bureaucracy" as "brainwashed," as they took management's side against their own workers, while their power base was cut out from under their feet. "John L. Lewis disregarded their general strike and announced instead that the union was for 'progress.' The working force in the mines was literally cut in half." When automation took hold in automobile manufacturing, "Reuther told the auto workers to consider 'the future' which would bring them a six-hour day … Meanwhile, there has been no change in the working day since the workers, through their own struggles over decades, won the eight-hour day."[28] This was a classic idealist mistake: "painting the future as it *should* be instead of speaking of what is." While Reuther promised better living conditions and increased leisure in an automated future, workers testified to the opposite. As one autoworker complained, "All Automation has meant to us is unemployment and overwork. *Both at the same time.*"[29] As Dunayevskaya unsparingly put it, "The workers don't go in for abstract argumentation on leisure and plenty at some future, unspecified, time."[30]

Around the time Dunayevskaya was analyzing worker resistance to automation, her collaboration with James was drawing to a close. Seeking a new interlocutor well versed in Hegel and Marx, she struck up a correspondence with Herbert Marcuse, the Frankfurt School philosopher who had since become ensconced in American academia. When Marcuse began his research for his classic analysis of advanced capitalism *One-Dimensional Man*, he requested materials on automation from

Dunayevskaya, who eagerly supplied him with a bibliography of contemporary texts, as well as a copy of the workers' newsletter she edited, *News and Letters*, with an extensive inquiry by Charles Denby on the impact of automation from the perspective of workers.[31]

Denby, a Detroit autoworker and editor at *Notes and Letters*, accumulated accounts from workers discussing new automation technologies, including those working on assembly lines and in mines, and even the white-collar workers struggling with new computer technologies. He was as unsparing in his analysis as Dunayevskaya had been in her writing on the miners' strike, detailing the brutal pace, strenuous physical and mental demands, and the strife of technological unemployment brought by the new machines.

Denby's investigations prompted workers to articulate visions of alternative working conditions, which repeatedly surface throughout the study. Of particular interest to Denby was the way automation obviated any mental investment in work. As he described it:

> What alienates a production worker is that he is driven to do work that is separated from his thinking ... Before Automation, when a major change was made and a new machine was introduced, they had to rely on the workers' knowledge and experience to get it working properly ... For a few weeks we felt like human beings working out the problems together and getting things organized and moving smoothly.[32]

Workers contrasted the anomie of the automated environment with the social ties and camaraderie they had developed previously.

> Some years ago, when workers had something to say about how fast they would work and the amount of help they felt they needed if the company wanted more production, the relations

among production workers were humanly close. They could help each other with their work. They worked in a way which would make it easy for every one in a group. Today Automation does not allow anyone to help another worker.[33]

Like Dunayevskaya, Denby was intrigued by the way the miners opposing automation were "answering their own questions by devising ways to unite thinking and doing."[34] Denby's colleague at *News and Letters*, factory worker Andrea Terrano, put it pointedly:

Why do people assume that Automation is the way people will want to work in a new society? Why do they assume that all that matters is that the workers will be in control? Will "being in control" of the machine lighten the work, or make it less boring? Won't work be something completely different? If work will be something different—tied up with life itself—it cannot be the same as Automation that uses men as part of its operations.[35]

Rather than rely on worker testimony, Marcuse depended instead on technical experts and credentialed philosophers. While Marcuse noted some of the problems with automation, and cited Denby, *One-Dimensional Man* provided an optimistic take on new production technology. Like James, he saw salutary effects in how automation organized workers. "The same technological organization which makes for a mechanical community at work also generates a larger interdependence which integrates the worker with the plant," he wrote, imagining a potential for a more social and participatory relationship toward work in the factories.[36] And in a personal translation of a quotation from Marx's *Grundrisse*, Marcuse provides one of the earliest appearances in English of the "Fragment on Machines": *One-Dimensional Man* was published in 1964, almost a decade before the English translation of the

Grundrisse. Marcuse's reading of the fragment as presaging a moment of full automation gives his interpretation a decidedly "luxury communism" flavor: "Complete automation in the realm of necessity would open the dimension of free time as the one in which man's private and societal existence would constitute itself. This would be the historical transcendence toward a new civilization."[37]

In her review of *One-Dimensional Man,* Dunayevskaya criticized Marcuse for misreading Denby's work, and for folding it into his argument that workers had been incorporated into a totally administered society. Marcuse, she wrote, "leaves out entirely the central point of the pamphlet, the division between the rank and file and the labor leadership in their attitudes toward Automation."[38] Relying on technical analyses of automation led Marcuse to the belief that there was no longer significant opposition at the point of production. Instead, Marcuse should have heeded the words of the workers situated at just this point. Dunayevskaya notes, "It is a question of the voices one hears, the sights one sees, the feelings one experiences depending on which side of the production line you stand."[39] After all, as Denby himself put it, "there is an expression used by miners which is as old as mechanization in the mines. It is simply this: 'A man has no business on a machine who can't break it down any time he wants to.'"[40]

The *News and Letters* group's diagnosis of worker resistance to automation remained somewhat abstract, without a concrete vision of what utopian, or simply more equitable, productive relations might be. However, they highlighted a number of points important to a Marxist theory of social and technological change. Foremost, they held steadfast to the belief that the key to socialist transformation lay not in technological development, but in the struggle of workers, including struggles against new technologies, through which workers would discover new forms of organization and raise deeper political questions. And through their contact with other workers in struggle, they uncovered a desire for autonomous, productive, and sociable working relationships—not simply, as Marcuse would have it, more leisure time.

The Docks

Perhaps nowhere was that desire for creative and social working relations stronger, or more fully realized, than among the notoriously militant and independent workers at the ports of entry. Stan Weir's memoir of life as a Bay Area dockworker is a moving illustration of the culture of the longshoremen, where hard-fought autonomy encouraged creativity, individuality, and even eccentricity. According to economic historian Marc Levinson, the irregularity of work also meant that dockworkers could, if they wished, take time off for their own activities. The danger, precarity, and difficulty of the work produced a unique culture with powerful bonds of solidarity and an "us against the world" mentality. "Dockworkers saw themselves as tough, independent men doing a very tough job."[41] Longshoremen dressed as they wished, told jokes, and discussed politics and philosophy. As Weir recounts, "There is presently a nationally recognized small press book club operated by a lone San Pedro longshoreman. There are teachers, artists, realtors, and poets."[42] Author Eric Hoffer worked on the San Francisco docks for twenty years, during which time he wrote acclaimed books such as *The True Believer*, a social psychology of mass movements. E.P. Thompson's description of the autodidactic and creative culture of the pre-factory weavers of northern England immediately comes to mind: "Every weaving district had its weaver-poets, biologists, mathematicians, musicians, geologists, botanists."[43]

And like those weavers, longshoremen knew that technology was a death knell for their culture of intimacy and independence. As technology saturated the docks, it transformed the structure of work, and indeed the ports themselves. The shared experiences that bonded longshoremen together in solidarity were balkanized, spread to several different professions and different unions:

> The machinery has caused the boundaries of the longshore industry to become fluid and without exact shape. The maintenance of longshore machinery no longer requires the skills of marine riggers so much as it does that of electricians and truck mechanics. The shoreside cranes are of the type normally run by members of the Operating Engineers Union. The enormous amount of rolling stock that moves containers in the marshalling yards requires the performance of labor that little resembles traditional longshore work. The Teamsters Union has already claimed a portion of this work with some success.[44]

This was the impact of "containerization," the technological standardization of shipping by enclosing all cargo into uniform metal crates. Containers were intermodal: crates could be loaded, by crane, directly onto or off of ships via trains and trucks. This meant the end of the laborious loading and unloading cargo by hand, piece by piece, a process so time-consuming that, in the words of journalist Marco d'Eramo, "Ships therefore spent more time in port than at sea."[45] Containerization meant much less need for workers, something the longshoremen understood immediately. The major dockworker unions went into negotiations.

The result, on both the West Coast and the East, was the surrender of control of the labor process to the shippers. Long-standing regulations were simply discarded in order to intensify work. According to Weir's account, "On the first day that the mechanization agreement went into effect, hold men found themselves working sling loads of hand-handled cargo that were double or more the weight of those that had been hoisted in and out of hatches the previous day."[46] Output at the docks increased, but at great human cost. "As productivity climbed, so did accident rates. Between 1958 and 1967, U.S. waterfront employers reported a 92.3 percent increase in the number of workers' compensation cases 'despite efforts to engineer problems out of the workforce.'"[47] Higher accident rates stemmed from workers' loss of control of the pace and style of their jobs. The automation contracts negotiated between the International Longshore and Warehouse Union (ILWU) and the Pacific Maritime Association gave up previously negotiated work rules, in particular the 2,100-pound limit on each load of cargo hoisted out of a ship. This strict rule had previously prevented attempts to speed up dock work.[48] While union leadership attempted to channel unrest into wage demands, resistance periodically broke out among the rank and file over working conditions, particularly the physical stresses and the mindlessness of automated work.

Containerization completely upended the dock system. Not only were fewer dockworkers required for the containerized ports, but, by drastically reducing loading and unloading times, and therefore making the shipment of goods dramatically less expensive, fewer ports were needed; many cities, including New York, saw their waterfronts and their associated communities decimated in just a few years.[49] But the revolution didn't stop at the docks. As the transportation of goods was no longer cost-prohibitive, manufacturing could be located wherever labor costs were lowest. It could also be centralized, since there was little need to locate production close to consumption. Containerization was the essential precondition for what has become known as globalization, where production is scattered along far-flung international supply chains.

Like David Noble, Weir notes that containerization was not driven solely by industry needs for efficiency, but also by military order: "The necessary planning for the automation of longshoring and shipping began in 1952 at the initiative of the Pentagon and maritime employers, under the auspices of the

National Academy of Sciences."[50] Military contracts to supply the burgeoning invasion force in Vietnam provided commercial shippers with further leverage over intransigent dockworkers during the 1960s. Indeed, without containerization, Levinson argues that "America's ability to prosecute a large-scale war halfway around the world would have been severely limited."[51] In fact, the Vietnam War was instrumental to early processes of globalization: after dropping their materiel in Da Nang, container ships stopped off in Japan to fill up with electronics before returning to the West Coast.[52]

Martin Glaberman, a Johnson-Forest member and auto-worker, keenly observed the effects of automation in industries that had the highest levels of militancy: mining, dock work, and automobile manufacture. "It should be clear," he wrote, "that the problem does not lie in the inability of the unions to find a solution to such problems as automation. They have imposed a solution on the workers." In response to union capitulation, workers took matters into their own hands. As Glaberman wryly noted:

> The workers have no use for the contract and no illusions that contracts can be improved. They have turned to doing their own "negotiating" on the shop floor. Assembly lines have a way of breaking down—and who is to say that the bolt which jammed the line was not dropped accidentally? Who is to know that the warning lights which signal the stoppage of the line were not burned out but merely unscrewed to add a few minutes to the time it takes to repair the line?[53]

This turn to sabotage was, for Glaberman, the germ of new and creative forms of struggle occurring on the shop floor, "a search for new forms of organisation that are adequate for their needs."[54] By many accounts, this search continues on the docks today. In 2011, for instance, ILWU members in Seattle and Tacoma damaged freight cars, dumped grain, and attacked windows with baseball bats during a contract dispute.[55] In Vancouver in 2013, United Grain locked out ILWU dockworkers in response to alleged attacks on its equipment: "The deliberate introduction of a metal pipe approximately two feet long into [the] conveyor system as well as the intentional introduction of a sand and water mixture into the railcar progressor."[56] These techniques draw upon a current of struggle stretching back decades, opened up by the introduction of automation.

Black Workers and Automation

The recomposition of the workforce during the Second World War meant tentative gains in the workplace for black workers, as ramped-up wartime production and a massive draft meant that employers were desperate for labor. However, racism and segregation were still the rule. Confined to the worst and lowest-paying jobs and cut off from training programs and apprenticeships that might have provided a greater skill level and more job security, black workers were often first in line when layoffs came. They were therefore disproportionately targeted by the midcentury push for automation, which destroyed "low-skill" jobs, and thus increased black unemployment.

While the civil rights movement is often remembered for its dramatic confrontations over the desegregation of civil society, from lunch counters to buses to public schools, labor politics were also a central concern. Indeed, A. Philip Randolph's plans for a national march on the capital to desegregate the defense industry pushed Roosevelt to do just that in 1941. Two decades later, Martin Luther King Jr. and Bayard Rustin organized the March on Washington for Jobs and Freedom. As the integration of the workplace was a major goal, postwar civil rights leaders viewed automation, and its disruptive impact on labor markets, as a potential problem for their movements. In a 1961 address to the AFL-CIO, Martin Luther King Jr.

declared, "Labor today faces a grave crisis. In the next ten to twenty years automation will grind jobs into dust as it grinds out unbelievable volumes of production." King understood that automation was a weapon to be used against organized labor: "This period is made to order for those who would seek to drive labor into impotency by viciously attacking it at every point of weakness." And the unions' only chance to take control of the course of automation was to forge a common cause with the civil rights movement: "The political strength you are going to need to prevent automation from becoming a Moloch, consuming jobs and contract gains, can be multiplied if you tap the vast reservoir of Negro political power." [57] Malcolm X, in contrast, argued that the threat of automation justified a separatist strategy. "At best," he cautioned, "Negroes can expect from the integrationist program a hopeless entry into the lowest levels of a working class already disenfranchised by automation." [58]

The link between automation and the fate of black Americans drew increasing interest over the decade. In 1964, an assortment of figures from the American left and intelligentsia —including Students for a Democratic Society leaders Tom Hayden and Todd Gitlin, democratic socialists Michael Harrington and Irving Howe, anti-nuclear activist Linus Pauling, cyberneticist Alice Mary Hilton, civil rights leader Bayard Rustin, and erstwhile Johnson-Forest Tendency associate James Boggs—formed the "Ad Hoc Committee on the Triple Revolution." The committee issued a statement in the influential New Left magazine *Liberation*, and sent a copy to President Lyndon B. Johnson, warning of oncoming destabilization at the hands of three interconnected trends: automation (referred to as "cybernation"), the replacement of conventional weapons with nuclear ones, and the civil rights movement.

This "triple revolution" posed an existential challenge to US institutions—one that would require dramatic policy shifts if it was to be overcome, well beyond the ambitions of Johnson's War on Poverty. Without a radical restructuring of the economy in the face of automation, the civil rights demand for inclusion could not be met (and the reduced need for standing armies meant the military would not sop up the surplus, as it had decades earlier). The Ad Hoc Committee's statement pronounced: "The Negro is trying to enter a social community and a tradition of work-and-income which are in the process of vanishing even for the hitherto privileged white worker. Jobs are disappearing under the impact of highly efficient, progressively less costly machines." If nothing was done, millions would be immiserated: "A permanent impoverished and jobless class is established in the midst of potential abundance."[59]

However, out of this doomsday scenario emerged the potential for redemption through a planned embrace of new technology by government policy makers. The Ad Hoc Committee concluded on an optimistic, fully automated note:

> We assert that the only way to turn technological change to the benefit of the individual and the service of the general welfare is to accept the process and to utilize it rationally and humanely. The new science of political economy will be built on the encouragement and planned expansion of cybernation. The issues raised by cybernation are particularly amenable to intelligent policy-making: Cybernation itself provides the resources and tools that are needed to ensure minimum hardship during the transition process.[60]

The document went on to enumerate the incredible scale of the measures required: more education spending, a large public works program, affordable housing, investment in mass transit, and a more egalitarian tax system that would redistribute income. While Johnson's advisor Lee C. White assured the committee that the president would establish a commission to study the issue, the manifesto failed to have its intended effect, and the backlash was swift. "Guaranteed Income Asked for All, Employed or Not," scoffed the *New York Times*,[61] while Daniel Bell, the prominent social theorist and political commentator, quibbled with the economics.[62] Ultimately, the letter, however cogently argued, failed to make an impact on policy makers, who opted to do nothing.

Economists continued to study the issue. Herbert Northrup, a longtime researcher on black labor, wrote in 1965:

> An important factor in the Negro unemployment problem was industry's substitution of machinery for unskilled labor ... Negroes laid off as a result of these developments and young Negroes who found that industry was no longer hiring the unskilled became significant proportions of the hardcore, long-term unemployed.[63]

In *Monopoly Capitalism*, Paul M. Sweezy and Paul A. Baran's 1966 analysis of capitalist political economy, the pair of Marxist economists agreed that automation had severely circumscribed the economic prospects of African Americans working in manufacturing: "Since 1950 ... with unskilled jobs disappearing at a fantastic rate, Negroes not qualified for other kinds of work found themselves increasingly excluded from employment altogether."[64] By the early 1960s, black unemployment was double that of white unemployment. While Baran and Sweezy were eager to place the blame for black hardship on the capitalist system as a whole, rather than its technology, they admitted that "within the framework of this society technological trends, because of their differential impact on job opportunities, can rightly be considered a cause and undoubtedly the most important cause, of the relative growth of Negro unemployment."[65] Ernest Mandel used this political economic framework to explain growing black radicalization: "The rapid decline in the number of unskilled jobs in American industry is the nexus which binds the growing negro revolt, especially the revolt of negro youth, to the general socio-economic framework of American capitalism."[66]

Radical black intellectuals dealt with automation as a serious social problem for black workers and liberation movements. Robert L. Allen's widely read study of 1960s black radicalism, *Black Awakening in Capitalist America*, sounded a dire note. "Not only is the economic situation of the masses of blacks grim," he wrote, "but the prospects are that it will not improve, rather it will deteriorate. This is due partly to the unregulated impact of automation."[67] Allen predicted the continued degradation of the social power and conditions of black people over the next decades, a prediction as stunning for its pessimism (his book was published in 1969, a high-water mark for US radicalism) as its prescience.

For sociologist Sidney Willhelm, writing in 1970, automation threatened to upend the achievements of the civil rights movement: "Though widespread opinion strongly supports the view that integration is likely, many signposts indicate eventual isolation of the Negro people, an isolation made possible by the changing technology of automation."[68] According to Willhelm, for most of US history black Americans occupied a contradictory location—one in which they were subject to racist abuses but simultaneously required as a superexploited population of laborers. However, the replacement of human labor with machines would undermine black workers' economic function. "If machines eventually accomplish what man has in fact developed up to this point," he remarked, "then perhaps people will become surplus baggage? But, then, how long will we tolerate one another as surplus baggage?"[69] Willhelm foresaw a dire situation where, bereft of economic utility, black Americans would be subject to unchecked racism and deepening segregation:

The Negro is losing out because he is losing out in the technological development of American society; *White America can,
for the first time, easily bear the economic costs for implement-
ing its racial values to the point of excluding the Negro race.*
More specifically, the developing outcast position of the Negro
is in keeping with the technological configuration of White
America's economic interests.[70]

In raising the specter of black people as an unneeded "surplus
baggage" to the economy, Willhelm did not hesitate to suggest
genocidal outcomes: "Where economic competition against
whites once contributed to race relations, now the Negro
competes against the machine; the first competition resulted
in white extortion, the second brings in its wake the Negro's
obliteration."[71]

This was an analysis that the Black Panther Party took into
the heart of their organizational philosophy, which was geared
toward organizing the "lumpenproletariat": the class cut off
from wage labor. As Eldridge Cleaver spelled out, the lumpen,
which included those "who have been displaced by machines,
automation, and cybernation," represented a real contradiction within the proletariat.[72] Indeed, machines were, in part,
responsible for this bifurcation. The polarization of skill meant
that "every job on the market in the American Economy today
demands as high a complexity of skills as did the jobs in the
elite trade and craft guilds of Marx's time."[73] This elitist
configuration had sapped a portion of the proletariat of its
revolutionary zeal, an elán that was now the preserve of the
technological outcasts. Huey Newton clarified Cleaver's points
in terms of a longer-range strategy:

In this country the Black Panther Party, taking careful note of
the dialectical method, taking careful note of the social trends
and the ever-changing nature of things, sees that while the

lumpen proletarians are the minority and the proletarians are the majority, technology is developing at such a rapid rate that automation will progress to cybernation, and cybernation probably to technocracy … If the ruling circle remains in power it seems to me that capitalists will continue to develop their technological machinery because they are not interested in the people … Every worker is in jeopardy because of the ruling circle.[74]

Meanwhile, black workers who remained on the factory lines formulated their own analysis of automation. Productivity had increased dramatically over the past decades, but while management credited the machines, these workers pointed to the dangerous speedups they had been subjected to, what they called, in the factories of Detroit, "niggermation."[75] The injuries and deaths—dozens a day, a casualty rate higher than in the Vietnam War—meant that workers understood the factory as itself a warzone. With their concerns over racism and new technology ignored by both management and established unions, black workers formed militant groups like the League of Revolutionary Black Workers and the Dodge Revolutionary Union Movement, successfully shutting down auto factories through wildcat strikes.

In the midst of the tumult of the 1960s, the most significant black radical groups placed a critique of technology at the center of their analysis and their politics. They recognized that the technological recomposition of the workforce would shape the fate of their struggles. In the 1972 update to the Black Panther Party's Ten-Point Program, the last point added "people's community control of modern technology" to the demands for "land, bread, housing, education, clothing, justice, peace."[76]

Feminism and Automation

New technology also came into focus for the women's movement, perhaps the most intellectually vibrant formation of the postwar period. Some women speculated that technology, by reducing the need for strength and skill in jobs, would have a leveling effect on the workplace, allowing women into positions that had been off limits to them. This perspective was questioned by feminist labor process theorists like Cynthia Cockburn, who directly studied the impact of technology on the gendered division of labor. As feminist researchers have continually found, rather than simply remove barriers, new technologies recomposed work in complex ways, often to the detriment of women. "Technology is far from neutral," Cockburn plainly states. "Industrial, commercial, military technologies are masculine in a very historical and material sense. They cannot readily be used in a feminine, nor even a sexless, mode."[77]

Indeed, in many cases, automation eliminated and degraded jobs already occupied by women. A case in point is the fate of telephone operators. A class of worker made up entirely of women, operators struggled for decades against increasingly mechanized working conditions, which concentrated more and more switchboard work among fewer and fewer workers while eliminating downtime. When operators joined unions, their core demands about the degraded quality of their work were cast aside, channeled instead into more traditional trade union demands. Historian Venus Green, a former telephone operator herself, documents how the bureaucratic trade union mentality meant ignoring the concrete demands of operators. "Higher wages, shorter hours, and union grievance procedures," she writes, "did not ameliorate the strictly supervised and relentless, machine-driven work pace from which operators suffered."[78]

Instead of taking operator demands seriously, union leadership praised automation for its promise of leisure. For instance, Communications Workers of America President Joe Beirne stated, "For ourselves, we welcome automation because we see in it a level for higher wages, longer vacations, shorter hours, and ultimately, greater security for ourselves and the American people."[79] If these beneficial effects were to come— and they largely were not—they would be at the expense of operators, who found themselves out of jobs. Green suggests sexism played a part in union indifference, and notes that the male leadership viewed the recomposition of telephone operation as beneficial to male workers, who could take new positions as technical supervisors over automated dialing machines. Those same machines put telephone operators out of their jobs, while removing autonomy over the pace of work from the women who remained.[80] Ultimately the only "long vacations" and "shorter hours" were those that accrued to the unemployed: the thousands of dues-paying women who lost their jobs.

Beyond the workplace, feminists analyzed and politicized the unwaged work of the housewife, the labor of social reproduction that was essential to capitalism but performed without remuneration. Here too was another area of life where technology promised to alleviate burdens and spread the gifts of leisure; and here too those promises went unfulfilled.

Homemaking had long been of interest to scientific management. In the best-selling 1948 memoir *Cheaper by the Dozen*, two of the twelve children of industrial engineer Frank Gilbreth, a fervent disciple of Frederick Taylor, recount humorous anecdotes of their father's home life. Gilbreth, the inventor of so-called time and motion studies, possessed an enthusiasm for order and efficiency so all-consuming that he made it the basis of his parenting style. In the Gilbreth home, no moment could be wasted. Baths were supplemented by German language lessons and clearing the table was done according to stopwatch. The book's comedic peak sees Gilbreth pressuring a doctor into performing tonsillectomies of all twelve progeny according to the apparent insights derived from his time and motion studies.[81]

While the book, and its successful 1950 film adaptation, play up Gilbreth's zeal for family-friendly laughs, sociologists Tilla Siegel and Nicholas Levis point out that it can also be read as a prescient depiction of how the rationalization of work quickly bleeds into the rationalization of the domestic sphere.[82] In fact, the most influential capitalists understood this connection well. Henry Ford, troubled by massive resistance to his new assembly line, knew he would need more than a high wage to coax workers into his factories. He would have to mold the worker's subjectivity far beyond the shop floor, what Antonio Gramsci recognized as "the need to elaborate a new type of man suited to the new type of work and productive process."[83] Creating this "new man" was the job of the Ford Sociological Department, who conducted interviews in the factory towns about the organization of workers' home life, collecting details on everything from alcohol consumption to sexual habits. Ford placed a heavy emphasis on the standardization of gender roles: the discovery of an employee's wife working outside the home could be grounds for dismissal.

Gilbreth and Ford's examples demonstrate that the project to rationalize the home has more in common with the needs of patriarchy and capitalism than the needs of women. This is precisely the argument Selma James and Mariarosa Dalla Costa make in *The Power of Women and the Subversion of the Community*, their 1975 manifesto for the Wages for Housework movement. In James and Dalla Costa's analysis, the result of Ford's project was a mutually beneficial arrangement between capitalism and patriarchy in the construction of the nuclear family. The nuclear family, they observed, compelled women into providing necessary labor that did not have to be compensated by capital, and the drudgery reproduced women's isolation and subjugation to the male wage earner. Therefore, "the maintenance of the nuclear family is incompatible with the automation of these services. To really automate them, capital would have to destroy the family as we know it." Because domestic labor is a relation of patriarchal power, technology will not liberate women. Instead, their time will be filled with more domestic work: "We all know the saying too well: you can always find work to do in a house." They conclude that it is instead feminism, not technology, that will liberate women from housework.[84]

Ruth Schwartz Cowan's 1983 *More Work for Mother*, one of the most acclaimed histories of domestic technology to emerge in the wake of the women's movement, confirms James and Dalla Costa on an empirical level. While official discourse —advertisements, news articles, patents—tell a story of an easier workload for homemakers, "when discussed by the people who actually did housework, or by the people who watched the people who were doing it, it seems not to have become one whit more convenient—or less tiring—during the whole of the century."[85]

Cowan, surveying domestic technology from 1860 to 1960, found that rather than relieve beleaguered housewives, domestic technologies tended to ease home activities traditionally performed by men. Innovations such as the gas cooking stove and the automatic flour mill freed men from chopping wood and grinding grain, allowing them more time to work outside the home. Meanwhile, women assumed a greater proportion of domestic labor: "You [the housewife] bore the whole burden of housework. For your husband and your children, the house became a place of leisure."[86] According to Cowan, one result of the mechanization of housekeeping was a dramatic reduction in the number of paid domestic laborers, with the concomitant extension of housekeeping duties for the woman of the home. The introduction of the washing machine replaced the reliance on professional laundresses—instead, the housewife could do the work for free. The mechanization of the work of social reproduction, in this account, serves to shore up a gendered division of labor, rather than reduce the time spent in toil. "The end result is that housewives, even of the most comfortable classes (in our generally now comfortable society) are doing housework themselves."[87]

Yet in spite of so many feminist scholars' affirmations that technology, both at work and at home, functioned to reinforce the gendered division of labor, the faith remained strong that these new developments could somehow undermine it. One of the most striking technophilic manifestos was Shulamith Firestone's *The Dialectic of Sex*, a work whose theoretical sophistication and prosodic brio have kept its influence alive for the half century following its publication. [88]

Firestone begins with the assertion that the oppression and exploitation of women—what she calls "sex class," which she argues is distinct from, and prior to, economic class—is rooted in the supposed biological differences between the sexes, specifically those related to human reproduction. The rigors of childbearing and childrearing fell to women, rendering them vulnerable and dependent on men, and thus leading to a subordinate position that was reproduced through the structure of the family.[89] However, biology, in her view, was not destiny. For Firestone, new technologies of contraception and fertilization held out the potential to diminish the biological basis for sex class, though she was quick to point out that "new technology, especially fertility control, may be used against [women] to reinforce the entrenched system of exploitation." Hence the need for a thoroughgoing feminist revolution, modeled on the Marxist dictatorship of the proletariat, which would entail "seizure of control of human fertility—the new population biology as well as all the social institutions of childbearing and childrearing."[90] Indeed, according to Firestone, the eruption of the feminist movement was predicated on the existence of such technologies. "Feminism," she wrote, "is the inevitable female response to the development of a technology capable of freeing women from the tyranny of their sexual-reproductive roles."[91]

In this way, reproductive technologies come into conflict with the existing relations of reproduction—the family—and thus begins the era of feminist revolution.

Firestone borrows from the structure of Marx's most technologically deterministic works, arguing that existing technologies are themselves neutral, becoming exploitative only in their specific uses. While Firestone carefully enumerated potential and actual abuses of contraceptive technology, such as the use of poor black and brown women as human test subjects, she maintained that abuses have to do with who is in power, rather than the technologies themselves. She likened her position to that of ecomodernists, who, rather than conserve nature, wanted to deploy technologies conscientiously to reshape it in egalitarian ways.

> As was demonstrated in the case of the development of atomic energy, radicals, rather than breastbeating about the immorality of scientific research, could be much more effective by concentrating their full energies on demands for control of scientific discoveries by and for the people. For, like atomic energy, fertility control, artificial reproduction, cybernation, in themselves, are liberating—unless they are improperly used.[92]

To be sure, romantic, and reactionary, notions of nature abounded in the counterculture—the "goddesses" that technology theorist Donna Haraway disdains in favor of cyborgs.[93] But the enthusiasm for technology also caused Firestone to make outsized claims. Even under capitalist patriarchy, Firestone believed in automation's progressive effects on gender relations:

> Job discrimination would no longer have any basis in a society where machines do the work better than human beings of any size or skill could. Machines thus could act as the perfect equalizer, obliterating the class system based on exploitation of labor.[94]

Yet this claim was flatly contradicted by feminist research into the labor process. Firestone's uncritical attitude to technology, ignoring the actually existing conditions of scientific and technological knowledge and use, is perhaps a case of bending the stick too far in the opposite direction.

The polemical edge of Firestone's work meant that it was fiercely contested among feminists. Many pointed out that, rather than liberate women from childbearing, reproductive technologies would relocate the locus of control over childbirth away from women and further toward the male-dominated fields of science and medicine. In 1985, the Feminist International Network of Resistance to Reproductive and Genetic Engineering, for instance, highlighted the connection between such technologies and imperatives for eugenics, medical experimentation, and population control, demanding, rather Luddishly, "a halt to the research and application of reproductive and genetic engineering in all its forms."[95] Contemporary critics such as Sophie Lewis rightly call attention to the pitfalls of FINRRAGE's stridency, including their deep attachment to gender essentialism, and their Manichean view of technology that ignores legitimate needs of poor women in the global South. As Lewis notes, abolitionist initiatives such as FINRRAGE's "perform opposition to commodification rather than to capitalism."[96] Yet despite these limitations, as feminist technology scholar Judith Wajcman argues, FINRRAGE rightly pointed to how patriarchal politics were embedded in the technologies themselves: for example, in the promotion of methods of in vitro fertilization that uphold the genetic ancestry of a heterosexual couple, rather than alternative forms of parentage that might destabilize the nuclear family.[97] The group's demands for "the recovery by woman of knowledge, skill and power that gives childbirth, fertility and all women's health care back into the hands of women" strikes at the heart of patriarchal domination of technology.[98]

In the postwar period, automation became a major political flashpoint for sundry radical movements, whether they focused on the docks, the factory, or the home. The political divisions were clear enough: workers repeatedly rebelled against these new technologies, while unions worked with capital to discipline unruly workforces to the machines. As radicalism intensified through the 1960s, capital accelerated its pace of technological change as part of a massive global restructuring around the various insurgencies breaking out across the postwar order. At the center of this change was a specific technology that the counterculture greeted with both fear and fascination: the computer.

4

High-Tech Luddism

The student movements of the 1960s were among the first to politicize the computer—at the time, massive mainframes that only governments, corporations, and universities could afford. Mario Savio, leader of the Berkeley Free Speech Movement, famously invoked opposition to "the machine" in his attacks on the bureaucratization and soullessness of the university and wider postwar society:

> There's a time when the operation of the machine becomes so odious, makes you so sick at heart that you can't take part! You can't even passively take part! And you've got to put your bodies upon the gears and upon the wheels, upon the levers, upon all the apparatus—and you've got to make it stop!

As historian Steven Lubar argues, Savio's poetic invocation was likely inspired by the university's information processing machine: in other words, a computer. By the 1960s, computer punch cards had become objects that represented people's contact point with bureaucracies ranging from the Census Bureau to the billing department of their local utilities. At UC Berkeley, students were required to fill out punch cards to register for classes. As such, Lubar notes, the cards were incorporated into movement actions:

> Berkeley protestors used punch cards as a metaphor, both as a symbol of the "system"—first the registration system and then

bureaucratic systems more generally—and as a symbol of alienation ... Punch cards were the symbol of information machines and so they became the symbolic point of attack.[1]

Students vandalized, burned, and otherwise destroyed punch cards designed for course registration; one student punched holes in a card to spell out the word "STRIKE."[2] As the student rebellion intensified in response to the Vietnam War, so too did actions against the computers residing on campuses. This development made perfect sense: Vietnam was, after all, the first computational war. Computers in the White House, the Pentagon, and eventually Saigon provided military planners with massive amounts of electronic data that determined the conduct of the war.[3]

The move toward strategies rooted in quantitative data collection and automated analysis represented a radical change in military culture—one resisted by the officer corps, who viewed warmaking as more art than science. Instead, this overhaul was led by the dictates of the civilian secretary of defense, Robert McNamara, who had previously used statistical analysis to turn around the fortunes of Ford Motor Company. Accordingly, the Pentagon judged military success in terms of quantitative metrics, such as "body count."

Even beyond the ambit of strategic calculation, the fighting of the war itself became computerized and automated, in what became known as "the electronic battlefield." General William Westmoreland revealed the concept, for several years a secret project at the Pentagon, at a public meeting with defense industry figures in October 1969:

> On the battlefield of the future, enemy forces will be located, tracked and targeted almost instantaneously through the use of data links, computer assisted intelligence evaluation, and automated fire control ...
>
> Today, machines and technology are permitting economy of

manpower on the battlefield, as indeed they are in the factory. But the future offers more possibilities for economy. I am confident the American people expect this country to take full advantage of technology—to welcome and applaud the developments that will replace wherever possible the man with the machine.[4]

As with the automation of factories during World War II, it was the Air Force, not the Army, who led the way on the electronic battlefield. Operation Igloo White knit together sensor arrays, communication networks, and aircraft to disrupt North Vietnamese movements along the Ho Chi Minh Trail. As Ian Shaw notes in his geographic study,

> Once a sensor detected a stimulus in the surrounding atmosphere—such as the sound of a passing truck, a vibration in the ground, the chemical "smell" of an NLF soldier, or even a change in light—it broadcasted a radio signal to nearby ground and air receivers, including Lockheed EC-121 planes.[5]

These "air receivers" were, as a pamphlet produced by the anti-war group Scientists and Engineers for Social and Political Action put it, "unmanned drones," part of an experiment with the intention of the eventual replacement of human pilots.[6] Bombers were directed to their targets by computer algorithms, and even the release of bombs was often automatic.[7]

The automation of war, as with the automation of industry, was an important means to reassert control over rebellious rank-and-file soldiers in Vietnam. As the anti-war movement successfully spread to the Army, soldiers increasingly refused to fight, sabotaged equipment, staged disruptive protests, and even murdered their commanders. Morale was in a state of collapse. However, the replacement of ground troops with aerial bombardment, itself increasingly automated, removed insurrectionary troops from the equation, prolonging the conflict.

The conclusion of many anti-war groups was that such automation was as much a political strategy as it was guided by military prerogatives.[8]

Much of the military computing projects' research and development, along with the data processing, relied on university computer science and engineering departments, which were thus drawn into anti-war struggles. Groups like the Union of Concerned Scientists, Science for the People, and Computer People for Peace formed to agitate within the scientific professions against collaboration with US militarism. And student movements intensified the targeting of computers, engaging in confrontations that went far beyond the playful tampering with punch cards. As the *Old Mole*, a student publication based in Cambridge, Massachusetts, put it in a 1969 article, demurely headlined "Let's Smash MIT":

> MIT isn't a center for scientific and social research to serve humanity. It's a part of the US war machine. Into MIT flow over $100 million a year in Pentagon research and development funds, making it the tenth largest Defense Department R&D contractor in the country.[9]

The mass shooting by National Guardsmen of protestors and bystanders at Kent State on May 4, 1970 ignited furor on campuses across the United States. Computers were often a target. On May 7, student demonstrators briefly occupied Syracuse University's computer center.[10] A few days later, on the heels of a tumultuous week of campus protests, activists took over a computer lab at the University of Wisconsin, destroying a mainframe in the process.[11] At NYU, as well, 150 protestors broke down doors and occupied the computer lab. They abandoned the occupation after two days, rigging the mainframe with improvised napalm connected to a slow-burning fuse. Two math professors managed to extinguish the fuse before the explosives went off; an assistant professor and a graduate teaching assistant were later arrested in connection with the incident.[12] At Stanford, the Computation Center was set ablaze, though without serious damage. Months later, in early February 1971, activists again targeted the center, giving speeches and distributing flyers calling for the divestment of Stanford computer resources from Defense Department activities. One speech highlighted the tactical value of targeting the computer:

> I'm not even going to talk about a strike. It doesn't matter either way. But what, I think that it's apparent that the place that has to be hit, and has to be hit hardest and can be hit not only here but in every college campus and in every city in the country are the computer centers. Computer centers are the most vulnerable places anywhere … It could mean just an hour delay. It could mean a day delay. It could mean a week delay. It could be a month delay or a year delay. Nobody knows. It's dependent upon what's destroyed in just that power shortage. What's destroyed in core storage. What's destroyed as to the records. What could be destroyed in the tape reserve rooms by the temperature going too high. Nobody knows.[13]

The Computer Takes Over

As the 1970s rolled on, protests fizzled out, and radical energies often flowed away from confrontation with the state and toward countercultural practices. Some of these practices took extreme anti-technology stances; others began to rehabilitate the computer as an object for personal liberation, a view that would become increasingly hegemonic in the marketing of home computers, and later, the internet.[14] But beyond the roiling energies of the anti-war movement and their aftermaths, computers were part of another, deeper restructuring in the world of work.

97

Harry Braverman's classic analysis of machines and the labor process, *Labor and Monopoly Capital*, concluded with a sustained examination of this transformation. Braverman saw computers as having a Taylorist effect, similar to that of the introduction of automation in factory work:

> Once computerization had been achieved, the pacing of data management became available to management as a weapon of control. The reduction of office information to standardized "bits," and their processing by computer systems and other office equipment, provides management with an automatic accounting of the size of the workload and the amount done by each operator, section or division.[15]

As in the factory, Taylorism in the office sought to divide knowledge from execution, routinizing and deskilling the more autonomous and affective features that had characterized office work. Unlike in the factory, this division served to increase physical toil, rather than decrease it, as workers became appendages of tabulating and copying machines. A 1960 International Labour Organization report documented complaints among white collar workers of "muscular fatigue, backache, and other such ills as a result of the unaccustomed strain of operating machines."[16] And Ida Hoos's *Automation in the Office*, published in 1961, documented workers complaints about the overwork that accompanied this change. According to one of Hoos's informants, "The categories of jobs which have disappeared are those which require skill and judgement. Those remaining are the tabulating and key punching operations, which become even simpler, less varied, and more routinized as work is geared to the computer."[17]

Braverman's 1974 synthesis touched off a debate about the nature of what was termed the "white collar proletariat." Would the deskilling of office work transform the consciousness of what Nicos Poulantzas had identified, in his theorizing on class, as "the new petty bourgeoisie," turning docile typists and college-educated professionals into militants organizing against management? Often waged from the heights of theoretical abstraction, the debate was ultimately inconclusive. Instead, it would be a business school ethnographer who provided some of the most pertinent phenomenological observations on the computerized restructuring of work.

Shoshana Zuboff, a social scientist conducting ethnographic research in factories and workplaces in the early 1980s, was well positioned to observe the changes in industrial labor processes wrought by the implementation of computers. While not a Marxist herself, Zuboff recognized the technology as a flash point for class struggle. "The new technological infrastructure," she wrote, "becomes a battlefield of technique, with managers inventing novel ways to enhance certainty and control while employees discover new methods of self-protection and even sabotage."[18]

Zuboff viewed the new wave of computerization as containing two intertwined qualities. As work processes were automated by computerized technologies, they followed the dictates of classical Taylorism: management used machines to reorganize parts of the labor process where workers had accumulated a modicum of control. But at the same time it was automated, work was also "informated" by computers, which produced a real-time record of the labor process in the form of data. As she observed, "The programmable controller not only tells the machine what to do—imposing information that guides operating equipment—but also tells what the machine has done—translating the production process and making it visible."[19]

In turn, the informating of the labor process had two related effects. On the one hand, it altered the texture of work itself: its embodied qualities, its entire phenomenology for the worker. Skill in labor had previously been defined by the wisdom earned through physical repetition, a kind of tacit knowledge rooted in accumulated bodily practice that was impossible for many workers to verbalize, no matter how experienced. However, with the introduction of machines, and especially computer interfaces, to replace worker skill, jobs became a set of abstract instructions that workers had to cognitively interpret and understand, rather than a set of embodied tasks.

Because the texture of these new labor processes was mental rather than physical, workers in such environments could not be managed using the old methods—ones that had depended on the discipline of their bodies, their physical movements. In order to manage workers in the informated workplace, managers needed to discipline *minds*, so that workers' values and desires better aligned with the needs of the company. "As the work that people do becomes more abstract," Zuboff noted, "the need for positive motivation and internal commitment becomes all the more crucial."[20] How would workers internalize management prerogatives in such a way? Her perceptive conclusion was that the very same computer also provided a detailed account of each worker's behavior and the overall labor process to management, fulfilling the wildest fantasies of past generations of scientific managers. And more than a management tool, computerization transformed the workplace into a panopticon as described by Michel Foucault, where an environment of total surveillance impels the internalization of the dictates of power. Rendered as data, power becomes objective, a fact no one can argue with. As one worker told Zuboff,

> With these systems, there is no doubt. The results are the truth. They bring the truth to management. This means managers can really see what is happening, and they have to buckle down and focus on problems. It creates joint awareness. We end up working together more than fighting over what really happened.[21]

Yet while computers restructured many of the affective flash points of workplace clashes, they could not completely eradicate conflict between workers and management. In the digital panoptic workplace, struggle took on a subversive character, what workers termed "passive resistance," centered around obfuscation, invisibility, and, above all, manipulation of the computer. With the right passwords, numbers could be fudged; even when slacking could be detected, blaming computer error became a popular and effective technique.[22]

Processing the World

Scattered moments of passive resistance to computers like the ones Zuboff observed were the direct concern of the idiosyncratic Bay Area magazine *Processed World*. Situated in the heart of the IT revolution of the early 1980s, *Processed World* sought to sharpen the ambivalence about new technology, to hone it into antagonism. According to its editors, the publication's two goals were "to serve as a contact point and forum for malcontent office workers (and wage workers in general), and to provide a creative outlet for people whose talents were blocked by what they were doing for money."[23] Accordingly, *Processed World* featured an increasingly lively letters-to-the-editor section, along with comics, parodies of advertisements, poetry, and an overall wry and ironic tone. Its emphasis on bottom-up resistance and grassroots creativity was inspired by the Situationist International, and followed their model of widening the critique of capitalism from traditional workplace struggles to the "banality, hypocrisy, conformism, and dullness everywhere"—a critique not simply of work, but of everyday life.[24]

Founded in 1981, when "Silicon Valley" evoked microchips instead of apps, *Processed World* was still rooted in the tribulations of the workplace, chronicling the "day-to-day experience" of the bewildering recomposition of office labor and offering early militant inquiries into the vicissitudes of IT work. As historian Steve Wright frames it, *Processed World* offered lengthy analyses of "the labor process, culture and behaviors—in other words, the class composition—of employees engaged with work with information and information technology."[25] By the authors' own admission, class consciousness in this milieu was low, and labor organization practically nonexistent. The goal of *Processed World* was, therefore, to investigate what tendencies existed, and, when possible, to spark the initial fires of worker resistance through a mixture of irreverent humor and detailed analysis of the experience of work. By providing a forum, one of *Processed World*'s most important interventions was simply to alert atomized would-be agitators of one another's existence. Said one anonymous letter writer: "I don't think I've been this grateful since I was first taught how to read!"[26]

Processed World's most notorious essay hearkened back to the controversial IWW tracts of the 1930s. "Sabotage: The Ultimate Video Game," written by an office worker under the nom de plume "Gidget Digit," extols the virtues of machine breaking. "The urge to sabotage the work environment," she muses, "is probably as old as wage-labor itself, perhaps older." Digit proceeds to connect this archaic desire with the new technological apparatus of the office, its "new breakable gadgets" of computer terminals and fax machines: "Designed for control and surveillance, they often appear as the immediate source of our frustration. Damaging them is a quick way to vent anger or to gain a few extra minutes of 'downtime.'"[27] As a grateful reader subsequently wrote to the magazine, "I will leave it to the theoreticians to argue about the dialectical nuances of sabotage. Basically, there is one overwhelming reason to do it: it makes you FEEL GOOD."[28]

But Digit goes beyond describing such vandalism as a momentary atavism, however pleasurable it may be to the smasher. She theorizes it as one component of the continuous struggle in the office; in this sense, machine breaking is an ingredient in the roiling stew of class composition:

Sabotage is more than an inescapable desire to bash calculators. It is neither a simple manifestation of machine-hatred nor is it a new phenomenon that has appeared only with the introduction of computer technology. Its forms are largely shaped by the setting in which they take place. The sabotage of new office technology takes place within the larger context of the modern office, a context which includes working conditions, conflict between management and workers, dramatic changes in the work process itself and, finally, relationships among clerical workers themselves.[29]

This context was, according to Digit, part of a restructuring of work away from manufacturing to "the dazzling information sector." Even before personal computers had entered homes, Digit recognized the snake oil sold by techno-optimists about the flexible work routines of the digital future, seeing, like Zuboff, the surveillance potential of the new work technologies. "In fact," she observes, "rather than freeing clerks from the gaze of their supervisors, the management statistics programs that many new systems provide will allow the careful scrutiny of each worker's output regardless of where the work is done."[30]

Digit follows a Bravermanian line: computers, as the latest feature of automation, fragment and reorganize work to reassert managerial control. In other words, they will decompose "the type of work cultures ... that contribute to the low productivity of office workers" by undermining insubordinate practices like personal use of copiers and phones, coming in late, goofing off on the clock, and playing pranks. Digit predicts this control will extend into everyday life as information technology penetrates leisure through video games, home shopping, and cable television, providing expanded options at the expense of autonomous and creative free time. In her words, "The inhabitants of this electronic village will be allowed total autonomy within their personal 'user ID's,' but they are systematically excluded from taking part in 'programming' the 'operating system.'"[31]

Digit's politicization of technology exposed a rift among the editors at *Processed World* regarding automation. Tom Athanasiou took a line very close to today's Full Automators: "Though automation threatened livelihoods by eliminating degrading jobs, there is nothing inherently bad about computer technology, in a different society, it could be used to improve our lives in all kinds of ways." Athanasiou went so far as to sketch a communist utopia where "people would work, study, create, travel and share their lives because they wanted to, for themselves and for others." With a nod to Chile's abortive Cybersyn economic management project, Athanasiou argued that "computers could match needs to resources and pinpoint potential surpluses and shortfalls," a logistical underpinning for a society of abundance freed of markets.[32] Editor Maxine Holz dissented from this position. While acknowledging positive aspects of computers, she argued that "the immediate results of widespread implementation of much of modern technology are disadvantageous to workers and others directly affected. I think it is important not to lose sight of the current reality of conditions created by these tools."[33] The role of *Processed World* was not to sketch utopias or possible futures. It was to document, and thereby coalesce, the actually existing struggles in the IT sector.

In spite of her diagnosis, in light of the widespread sabotage of office technology, of "a common desire to resist changes that are being introduced without our consent," Digit opposed Luddite destruction by groups such as the French Committee to Liquidate or Divert Computers. Instead, she argued a Situationist line of technological *detournement*, toward "the more positive aim of subverting computers."[34] We might see

Digit's response as an early endorsement of the hacker way: resistance within and through technology, rather than purely against it.

Hacker cultures have been ascribed all manner of politics, from liberal to libertarian, radical to reactionary. And to be sure, hackers have participated in political projects from all of these quarters.[35] But the technological politics of hackers are complicated and, somewhat surprisingly, often quite Luddish. To understand why this is, we have to look at one of the earliest examples of struggles for technological control undertaken by hackers: the free software movement.

High-Tech Luddites

It might seem counterintuitive, even paradoxical, to associate some of the most enthusiastic and skilled users of technology with weavers wielding large hammers against comparatively rudimentary machines. Popular representations of hackers, whether it's a young Matthew Broderick using a computer and telephone modem to alter his biology grade in 1982's *War Games* or the Guy Fawkes-mask-wearing hordes of Anonymous, portray digital devices and technical know-how as the source of their power. And so the image of the misfit cybercriminal has been gentrified into the eccentric Silicon Valley entrepreneur who unleashes his (yes, his) technological mastery to forever alter society. Rather than smash machines, hackers embrace them. And so they should be some of the least Luddish figures on the planet.

And yet, if we look at the content of hacker politics as practiced by actually existing hackers, a different picture emerges. Far from a celebration of technology, hackers are often some of its most critical users, and they regularly deploy their skills to subvert measures by corporations to rationalize and control computer user behavior. They are often Luddites to the core.

One of the earliest and most influential examples of hacker organization of Luddite resistance is the free software movement, led by maverick programmer Richard Stallman. As Stallman tells it, programmers routinely shared code in the early days when software had to be designed from scratch. "Whenever people from another university or a company wanted to port and use a program, we gladly let them," he explains in his manifesto *Free Software, Free Society*. "If you saw someone using an unfamiliar and interesting program, you could always ask to see the source code, so that you could read it, change it, or cannibalize parts of it to make a new program."[36] Sharing and copying code became an essential practice within the nascent computer hacker culture, and one that promoted pedagogy, autonomy, and productivity.

The growth of personal computing led to an increased need for software, leading to the emergence of software companies who sought to meet this demand by turning software into a commodity to be bought and sold, not crafted. However, the plans of entrepreneurs to sell individual copies of software to each user collided with the widespread practice of copying and sharing code, at that point already deeply embedded in the hobbyist cultures of early computing. In 1976, one of those entrepreneurs, Bill Gates, wrote a scathing letter to the hobbyist community: "Most of you steal your software. Hardware must be paid for, but software is something to share. Who cares if the people who worked on it get paid?"[37]

Under pressure from the software industry, the US Supreme Court ruled that computer code was subject to copyright, a decision that threatened the working conditions of programmers like Stallman, who regularly copied code in order to tinker with it. Suddenly, copying was a crime. In response, Stallman formulated a set of alternative software licenses, so-called copyleft, designed to protect the open sharing of source code. When a piece of software incorporates Stallman's GNU General Public license, it adopts two fundamental precepts:

users are permitted to view and modify the code, and any new programs built with that code must, in turn, follow the GNU license. Propelled by a dedicated base of hackers and tinkerers, Stallman's licenses contributed to the growth of a large and successful—even commercially so—ecosystem of so-called free software.

Free software is an example of a Luddite technology: an innovation in the interest of the preservation of practitioners' autonomy against the imposition of control over the labor process by capitalists. By "breaking" software copyright and challenging closed and proprietary business models connected to it, free and open-source software has helped preserve independent and craft-like working conditions for programmers for decades. In addition to launching important software projects, like the operating system Linux, the free software movement was instrumental in establishing nonproprietary coding languages as standard in the industry, which meant that skill development, rather than being controlled exclusively by large corporations, could be done through open community involvement.[38]

Free software's successful struggles also helped to politicize an antipathy for intellectual property rights that continues to mark digital culture. Why stop at code? Hackers moved from liberating software to doing so for all forms of media content, from games to music to films. In both their technologies and their social practices, these digital pirates have often embraced older ways of doing things, rather than technological accelerationism. Even well into the BitTorrent era, the loose confederation of elite digital piracy crews labeled "The Scene" still operated via File Transfer Protocol (FTP) servers, a technology that predates even the World Wide Web.[39] When Napster emerged, making file sharing a major concern for the culture industries, careful observers noted that its genius stemmed, not from technological wizardry, but from its throwback architecture:

Napster is, in some ways, something of a regression to the old days of the Internet. Mass usage of the Internet has meant that servers have to be used to house information. Napster, on the other hand, relies on communication between the personal computers of the members of the Napster community.[40]

In other words, Napster's peer-to-peer architecture more resembles the distributed computing of the bulletin board system–era of the 1980s than "the cloud" of today that tethers us to the servers of massive tech companies.[41]

Many of the conflicts that have shaped the history of the internet—over intellectual property, over privacy and surveillance, over corporate control—are usefully conceived as struggles over subsumption, similar in structure to the struggles of the weavers of the early 1800s. Time after time, skilled computer users have mobilized to protect their established autonomous ways of crafting, exchanging, and using digital artifacts, rather than behaving as corporations such as Microsoft would have wished. In the 1990s, the web was a province of amateurs and hobbyists. Firms generated revenue from providing access to the internet, but once there, user behavior ran free through what were mostly noncommercial spaces: unofficial fan webpages, lightly regulated forums, troves of freely available games and software. This was a period of formal subsumption, where general capitalist imperatives of commodity exchange reigned, but individual user behavior was uncontrolled. As the Brazilian left communist group Humanaesfera notes, "the physical infrastructure was privately owned," but "the social content which emerged from this physical infrastructure was beyond the reach of capital."[42]

This idyllic time came to an abrupt end when, after a period of rampant speculation, the so-called dotcom bubble burst, taking down trillions of dollars in wealth along with a host of early online business models. At the time, some commentators even mused that the internet itself was nothing but hype. But digital capitalism would not be stopped so easily. A new technique of networked accumulation emerged as surviving techies reorganized digital interfaces and infrastructures into what entrepreneur Tim O'Reilly branded as "Web 2.0."[43] O'Reilly realized that the replication of the storefront, à la infamous bubble victim Pets.com, was a failing strategy. Instead, Web 2.0 would leverage "architectures of participation," whereby "users pursuing their own 'selfish' interests build collective value as an automatic byproduct."[44] In other words, activity would produce data. This occurred through a restructuring of computing itself through the internet. O'Reilly identified Google as the epitome of this transformation. Rather than offer software for users to install on their personal computers, Google provided services remotely while its software ran on its own servers: "a massively scalable collection of commodity PCs running open source operating systems plus homegrown applications and utilities that no one outside the company ever gets to see," or what we now call "the cloud." In this way, Google could act as the "middleman between the user and his or her online experience," all the while collecting data from the users of its services.[45]

O'Reilly's rosy notion of "participation" captured the imagination of techno-optimist intellectuals like Clay Shirky and Henry Jenkins, who heralded the rise of a democratic popular culture of "participatory media" online in the form of blogs, remixes, and creative fandoms. But the real story was not so much the participation as that "automatic byproduct": the user data, which could be fed back into the system, fine-tuning it. The data could be used to rationalize online behavior, extending the duration of activity within a platform and rendering it ever more productive and valuable. This was not democracy, but the transformation of the web into a distributed machine for the capitalist production of value. For critics such as media theorist Mark Andrejevic, the "architectures of participation" of Web 2.0 were better understood as "digital enclosures" for data extraction.[46] Today, for most of us, all our online activity —from scrolling through social media to watching old music videos to shopping for socks—is tracked by dozens, sometimes hundreds, of companies, who then squeeze this activity into marketing data.

Shoshana Zuboff, the ethnographer who made such detailed observations of the rise of computation in the workplace, has moved to studying this "new logic of accumulation," what she calls "surveillance capitalism."[47] For Zuboff, surveillance capitalism (whose paradigmatic example is, like O'Reilly's, Google) unfolds from the dynamics at work in the informatization of the workplace, which has served not only to automate labor processes but to continually generate data about them. With Google, all user behavior—every word in an email, every search, every mapped commute—becomes information that further improves the system, which is ultimately focused on selling advertising. This data is the property of Google, hoarded by the higher-ups in a company and used to extract value, with nothing delivered to those who produced the data but Google's services. This asymmetry is at the heart of what Zuboff classifies as the extractive logic of surveillance capitalism: "the absence of structural reciprocities between the firm and its populations."[48]

Zuboff describes all this as a sharp break with prior arrangements of profit making. But surveillance capitalism is better understood as the deepening penetration of commodity exchange and work relations into everyday life. It is not simply that the relations between tech companies and the rest of us are extractive, rendering these corporations indifferent to our fates. Marxists, among others, have rarely thought it sufficient to rely on the good graces of corporations. They suggest, rather, that it is the *restructuring* of behavior in directions directly productive of commodities—data—combined with the inexorable pressures of austerity toward new varieties of "monetization," that we must confront. And rather than submit to the metaphor of a natural resource, which treats data as existing in a state of nature, we must contend with how it is produced by human activity that has been locked within technological apparatuses, governed by opaque contracts. The way users produce data thus begins to resemble capitalist labor relations.

How have hackers responded to this situation? For one, they have battled surveillance capitalism by developing technologies that enhance and protect user privacy. Since the real subsumption of user behavior relies on surveillance and tracking, these privacy applications are another kind of Luddite technology, one that attempts to return the web to its formally subsumed state of relatively autonomous creative activity. Social scientist Maxigas documents the use by hackers of one such instance, a browser extension called RequestPolicy. RequestPolicy blocks so-called cross-site requests: instances, such as with Google's embedded ads or data analytics tracking, where the website you're visiting incorporates content from another site without alerting you. Because contemporary websites are rife with such third-party content, RequestPolicy effectively smashes the web, making normal commercial pages impossible to navigate, what Maxigas terms "a retrograde attempt to rewind web history: a Luddite machine that, as they say, 'breaks' the essential mechanisms of websites."[49]

The so-called dark web, where you can buy everything from a hit of acid to a hit on your neighbor, is a perfect encapsulation of the Luddite ethos in high-tech cultures. The dark web runs on the Tor protocol, which obfuscates user activity by routing it through an anonymous distributed architecture. By shielding user activity from the gaze of tracking technologies, Tor prevents this activity from being vacuumed up as data, and thus decommodifies it. Of course, the dark web is not itself free of commodification: in fact, the purchase and sale of goods and services, often of the illegal variety, runs rampant. Thus the dark web is not a space without market exchange, but a space without surveillance capitalism. Petty commodity exchange, especially of the kind idealized by libertarian economic theories, carries on, but it does so in isolation from the mechanisms of consolidation that have affected the fate of the rest of the web.

Tor sites themselves bear an uncanny resemblance to the early web of the 1990s. Pages are individually maintained, crashing frequently. Old lore of the bulletin board system— hacking tutorials, drug stories, text files of the *Anarchist Cookbook* replete with dodgy recipes for homebrewed intoxicants and explosives—are everywhere. Search engines work poorly, if at all, and so navigation relies more heavily on crosslinking and word of mouth. Tor's use of proxy means that page loading times hearken back to dial-up speeds, thus favoring the simple and straightforward HTML web design of the era of noisy modems. With Tor, Luddite technologies lead to Luddite aesthetics.

Rather than leave technological development to entrepreneurs on the assumption that it can be taken over wholesale by leftist political formations, Richard Stallman and other Luddite technologists recognize that technology is itself a flash point of current struggles. Further, they demonstrate not only that struggles against technologies of subsumption can win, but that they can also illuminate a path of alternative technological development. Yet hacker culture is often suffused with elitism, an unfortunate side effect often found in meritocratic craft cultures. Few everyday users will have the technical understanding to use Tor; fewer still will deign to suffer through RequestPolicy's upending of the really subsumed web.

There is an urgent need to think about how Luddite technologies could reach and impact more internet users, beyond the most skilled enthusiasts, especially as more and more activity —in particular, work—moves into online spaces subject to the dynamics of surveillance capitalism.

The New Digital Automation

We are at a critical moment, one when digital technologies of automation, often referred to with buzzy vocabulary like "algorithms" and "AI," are poised to transform both work and governance—or so we are told. Drawing from the massive glut of digitized information, the "big data" produced from a generation of informated activities, these technologies promise to transform all manner of employment, impacting the careers of even highly trained professionals in fields such as law and medicine. While white-collar jobs in "knowledge work" were once the promise of a comfortable future, now technologists such as Kai-Fu Lee, former president of Google China, promise that white-collar jobs will go first. According to Lee, "The white collar jobs are easier to take because they're pure a quantitative analytical process. Reporters, traders, telemarketing, telesales, customer service, [and] analysts, they can all be replaced by a software."[50]

Of course, the "replacement" of workers by software has happened for decades, and continues apace, often with dismal results. Government bureaucracies were some of the first places where computers promised to increase efficiency and cut costs, which is why the objects on your computer hard drive are "files" organized into "folders."[51] Today, as state facilities respond to cost-cutting neoliberal austerity with algorithms and software packages, the results are nothing short of devastating. Political scientist Virginia Eubanks details how the incorporation of "cost-saving" software packages into public assistance offices has created what she calls the "digital poorhouse":

> The digital poorhouse deters the poor from accessing public resources; polices their labor, spending, sexuality, and parenting; tries to predict their future behavior; and punishes and criminalizes those who do not comply with its dictates. In

the process, it creates ever-finer moral distinctions between the "deserving" and "undeserving" poor, categorizations that rationalize our national failure to care for one another.[52]

Rather than revolutionize government bureaucracies, she observes, "automated decision-making in our current welfare system acts a lot like older, atavistic forms of punishment and containment. It filters and diverts. It is a gatekeeper, not a facilitator."[53] Even well-meaning government employees succumb to a system that fragments and rationalizes their labor process. Where social workers once tracked individual cases, familiarizing themselves with their charges and gaining valuable context for judging courses of action, automated systems fragment cases into tasks to be handled, bereft of history or context. The result is, as one caseworker puts it, dehumanizing: "If I wanted to work in a factory, I would have worked in a factory."[54]

Similar systems are proliferating throughout governments. According to law professor Frank Pasquale, the impact of automation on the legal system is potentially catastrophic: the effacement of human judgement by algorithms means the end of the rule of law. For example, the COMPAS (Correctional Offender Management Profiling for Alternative Sanctions) algorithm uses "predictive analytics" to provide sentencing guidelines for judges, a kind of risk assessment of defendants' likelihood to commit future crimes. Because the algorithm is a trade secret, its inner workings are closed off to the public: part of what Pasquale calls the looming "black box society." COMPAS essentially provides secret evidence not subject to challenge or cross-examination, completely upending due process.[55] As demonstrated by Cathy O'Neil, a mathematician turned social critic, tools such as predictive policing (PredPol) rely on data sets produced from woefully discriminatory law enforcement and justice systems, thereby entrenching existing biases and inequalities. In favoring efficiency over other values, such as fairness, algorithmic law and order amounts to the "industrial production of *unfairness*."[56]

But as we have seen, and as many workers have taken pains to articulate, automation never completely erases human labor. Kai-Fu Lee's prediction of total replacement of knowledge work is thus a profound exaggeration, as a report by the think tank Data & Society makes plain: "AI technologies reconfigure work practices rather than replace workers," while at the same time, "automated and AI technologies tend to mask the human labor that allows them to be fully integrated into a social context while profoundly changing the conditions and quality of labor that is at stake."[57] Investigating grocery store self-checkout, researchers found that Luddish customers hated and avoided the technology. In response, management cut staff to make lines so unbearable that customers gave up and used the machines instead. Even then, cashiers were still required to assist and monitor transactions; rather than reduce workload, the technologies were "intensifying the work of customer service and creating new challenges."[58] This is an example of what technology journalist Brian Merchant calls "shitty automation":

> If some enterprise solutions pitchman or government contractor can sell the top brass on the idea that a half-baked bit of automation will save it some money, the cashier, clerk, call center employee might be replaced by ill-functioning machinery, or see their hours cut to make space for it, the users will be made to suffer through garbage interfaces that waste hours of their day or make them want to hellscream into the receiver—and no one wins.[59]

Store customers understand that self-checkouts mean tasks have been sloughed off on them, what media scholar Michael Palm classifies as "consumer labor."[60] And so they take revenge, rebelling against the technological imposition of work. Theft is rampant at self-checkouts. Bandits share techniques on forums like Reddit: hit "Pay" to disable the bag scale and then bag more items; always punch in the code for the cheapest produce (usually bananas); when in doubt, just throw it in your bag and walk out. They also offer justification: "There is NO MORAL ISSUE with stealing from a store that forces you to use self checkout, period. THEY ARE CHARGING YOU TO WORK AT THEIR STORE."[61]

Consumer labor in self-checkouts is an example of how rather than abolishing work, automation merely proliferates it. By isolating tasks and redistributing them to others expected to do it for free, digital technologies contribute to overwork. Writer Craig Lambert uses the term "shadow work" to describe this common experience with digital systems. The term derives from Ivan Illich, who used it to describe the devalued but necessary activities often performed by women, from housework to shopping to commuting.[62] For Lambert, digital technology also intensifies shadow work in the waged portion of life. When new technologies "automate" positions away, remaining workers often feel the brunt of new tasks. He describes the "job-description creep" facilitated by new software packages. Where administrative staff may have once kept track of bureaucratic matters such as employees calling off work, now "absence management" software requires workers to handle it themselves. "I am not sure why it has become my responsibility to do data entry for any time away from the office," a software developer tells Lambert. "Frankly, I have enough to do writing code. Why am I doing HR's job?"[63]

Atul Gawande writes evocatively of the effect of digital shadow work on the medical profession. After the introduction of a new software system for tracking patients, Gawande, invoking the specter of Taylorism, describes the painful restructuring of his work, away from patients and toward more structured interactions with computers. "I've come to feel that a system that promised to increase my mastery over my work has, instead, increased my work's mastery over me," he writes. "All of us hunched over our screens, spending more time dealing with constraints on how we do our jobs and less time simply doing them." But fighting against this bureaucratization-by-software, leads, he argues, to escalating burnout rates in the medical profession, the prevalence of which strongly correlates to how much time one spends in front of a computer.[64] And Gawande's specialization, surgery, is part of another technologically mediated crisis: as more daily activities revolve around typing and swiping, manual dexterity has declined: future surgeons have lost their ability to cut and stitch patients.[65]

As technology critic Jathan Sadowski argues, much of what is hyped as a system of autonomous machines is actually "Potemkin AI": "services that purport to be powered by sophisticated software, but actually rely on humans acting like robots."[66] From audio transcription services disguising human workers as "advanced speech recognition software" to "autonomous" cars run by remote control, claims of advanced machine intelligence not only amount to venture capital–chasing hype, but actively obfuscate labor relations inside their firms. As writer and filmmaker Astra Taylor argues, such "fauxtomation" "reinforces the perception that work has no value if it is unpaid and acclimates us to the idea that one day we won't be needed."[67]

While artificial intelligence is frequently likened to magic, it regularly fails at tasks simple for a human being, such as recognizing street signs—something rather important for self-driving cars. But even successful cases of AI require massive amounts of human labor backing them up. Machine learning algorithms must be "trained" through data sets where thousands of images are manually identified by human eyes. Clever tech companies have used the unpaid activity of users for years to do this: whenever you solve a ReCaptcha, one of those image identification puzzles to prove you're not a bot, you are helping to train AI—likely designed by the Google service's inventor, computer scientist Luis von Ahn, who came up with the idea through a practically Taylorist obsession with the unproductive use of time: "We're reusing wasted human cycles."[68]

But free labor only goes so far in the current AI boom, and more reliable professionalized workers are needed to surmount what anthropologist Mary L. Gray and computer scientist Siddharth Suri describe as "automation's last mile." Getting AI systems to function smoothly requires astonishing amounts of "ghost work": tasks performed by human workers who are kept away from the eyes of users, and off the company books. Ghost work is "taskified"—broken down into small discrete activities, "digital piecework" that can be performed by anyone, anywhere for a tiny fee.[69]

The labor pool for ghost work is truly global, and tech companies have been eager to exploit it. Samasource, which specializes in training AI, specifically targets the world's slum dwellers as a cheap solution for the "boring, repetitive, never-ending work" of feeding information into machine learning systems. The company's workers are poorly paid, though it justifies this through the compulsory rhetoric of humanitarianism that proliferates in Silicon Valley. Samasource's late CEO, Leila Janah, admits that employing low-wage workers from Kibera, Kenya—Africa's largest slum—is a profitable strategy. But it is, she claims, also the moral choice, so as not to upset the equilibrium of their impoverished surroundings:

> But one thing that's critical in our line of work is to not pay wages that would distort local labour markets. If we were to pay people substantially more than that, we would throw everything off. That would have a potentially negative impact on the cost of housing, the cost of food in the communities in which our workers thrive.[70]

Janah's humanitarian efforts notwithstanding, Samasource's business model reveals the real impact of networked digital technologies on the world of work. Even in a world of resurgent nationalism and hardening borders, the internet has created a massive globalized reservoir of human labor power for companies to tap into, as much or as little as needed: the "human cloud."[71] In this cloud, no far-flung locale need remain independent from the world's most powerful corporations, and with intense competition, you have to be quick and compliant even to snatch a gig at all. And no moment may be left unproductive: jobs can be sliced down to microtasks, paid as piecework, or "gamified" so they aren't paid at all. This potential future of work has nothing to do with expanding leisure from "full automation." Quite the contrary: in this future, work seeps into every nook and cranny of human existence via capitalist technologies, accompanied by the erosion of wages and free time.

The ghost work of the human cloud may give the impression that low-wage gig workers are alleviating the burdens of the lucky few who manage to snag a comfortable career. But computer-facilitated taskification comes for us all. The fumbling medical students provide a dramatic example of what the saturation of everyday life with digital technology has wrought: the deskilling of everyday life. Ian Bogost, a media scholar and video game designer, observes that the proliferation of automated technologies, from self-flushing toilets to autocorrecting text messages, accelerate feelings of precarity and unpredictability. This is because rather than serve human needs, they force people to adapt to unpredictable and uncontrollable machine logic: "The more technology multiplies, the more it amplifies instability." In response, we develop arcane rituals that make the toilet flush at the right time, or muddle through another "autocorrected" message full of typos. It is not simply a romantic critique that technology separates us from the sensuality of the world (though, humorously, Bogost relishes a physical paper towel over a sensor-triggered air dryer). It is a practical one: the supposed convenience of automated everyday life is undercut by our lack of control, our confusion, and the passivity to which technology conditions us. "Like people ignorant of the plight of ants," he writes, "and like ants incapable of understanding the goals of the humans who loom over them, so technology is becoming a force that surrounds humans, that intersects with humans, that makes use of humans—but not necessarily in the service of human ends."[72] This is precisely what philosopher Nolen Gertz describes as the "in-order-to mindset":

> Modern technologies appear to function not by helping us achieve our ends but instead by determining ends for us, by providing us with ends that we must help technologies achieve. Thus the Roomba owner must organize their home in accordance with the maneuvering needs of the Roomba, just as the smartphone owner must organize their activities in accordance with the power and data consumption needs of the smartphone. Surely we buy such devices to serve our needs but, once bought, we become so fascinated with the devices that we develop new needs, such as the need to keep the device working so that the device can keep us fascinated.[73]

Some scholars of contemporary technologies describe them in terms of older needs—or rather, older compulsions. For instance, social psychologist Jeanette Purvis notes that Tinder, the dating platform that ranks among the most popular apps of all time, works through an interface that uses "the same reward system used in slot machines, video games and even during animal experiments where researchers train pigeons to continuously peck at a light on the wall." Users swipe through an endless supply of randomized potential mates, an infinitude that results in an incredible churn—1.4 billion swipes a day—and an overall lower satisfaction with dates.[74] So desperately hooked to swiping are Tinder users that competing services like Coffee Meets Bagel market themselves on providing *fewer* options. And as a kind of artistic immanent critique, some wags have started selling "The Tinda Finger," a disembodied rubber digit that spins on a motor attached to one's phone, thus automating the swiping process. "The idea is to maximize the potential for matches while you can spend your time focusing on other things": automation to spare us from the "convenience" of automation.[75]

Breaking Machines

The Tinda Finger gestures toward a widespread popular discontent with our algorithmic, automated world, and an impulse to mock, challenge, and even damage the most palpable symbols of our dazzling digital economy. This "techlash"—one of 2018's defining words according to the *Financial Times*[76]— has reached the upper echelons of the political and intellectual elite, who were eager for social media, hackers, and memes to shoulder the blame for atavisms like Trump and Brexit. But the high-level discontent has been simmering for a while: plaintive nostalgics like Sherry Turkle and Nicholas Carr have been popular in Silicon Valley for years. Their books about the internet making us stupid and uncommunicative sit comfortably on the shelves of tech executives who ferociously limit their children's screen time and send them to elite tech-free schools, even as they push Chromebooks and course-management software on the rest of us.[77]

In an effort to ride the crest of this negative ferment, a number of prominent Silicon Valley entrepreneurs and designers have issued their own mea culpas at the Frankenstein's monsters they've helped to create. Some have even reached for that favorite solution of the tech bourgeoisie: founding a nonprofit. Ex-Googler Tristan Harris's Center for Humane Technology, which promises to "to reverse human downgrading by inspiring a new race to the top and realigning technology with humanity," has pride of place among them. Rather than hook users for as much time as possible, activity on digital platforms should be, as the slogan goes, "time well spent." But, as Ben Tarnoff and Moira Weigel caution in a 2018 essay in the *Guardian*, such endeavors leave unchallenged the massive power and wealth of companies like Facebook, and more perversely, they may even represent a new direction for their business:

> In other words, "time well spent" means Facebook can monetise more efficiently. It can prioritise the intensity of data extraction over its extensiveness. This is a wise business move, disguised as a concession to critics. Shifting to this model not only sidesteps concerns about tech addiction—it also acknowledges certain basic limits to Facebook's current growth model. There are only so many hours in the day. Facebook can't keep prioritising total time spent—it has to extract more value from less time.[78]

In other words, this is the transition from absolute surplus value, based on the extension of time spent producing data for Facebook, to relative surplus value, where time spent on Facebook is rendered more productive. Tech humanism is not about liberating people from digital capitalism, but about extending its reach, impelling users into more profitable activity: quality time to turn into quantitative value.

Unfortunately, the romantic nostalgia for face-to-face conversations or a retreat to humanist values and meaningful behavior, so often prescribed as a way out, lacks both the antagonism and the generalizability that will be needed if we are to break out of digital dystopias. The strategy of refusal pursued by the industrial workers of old might be a more promising technique against the depression engines of social media; as media scholar and activist Trebor Scholz notes, organized boycotts of Facebook date back to 2010.[79] Polling research indicates massive dissatisfaction with the platform, with over 40 percent of Facebook users taking extended breaks or quitting.[80] A final break is difficult to achieve: Pew found that social media use hasn't changed much,[81] though young people are increasingly trying to escape surveillance capitalism. Marketers warn: "significant cracks are beginning to show" when it comes to Generation Z and social media.[82] When one goes professional with their social media presence, as with the phenomenon of product-endorsing "influencers," the effects are exacerbated. YouTuber burnout videos are such a verifiable trend that YouTube commissioned one of its platform's creators to craft instructional mental health videos. But therapist Katie Morgan suffers from the same affliction she's trying to treat, the pressure to constantly perform and create: "I always feel like I should be working, or that they're counting on me."[83]

Refusal is only one form of resistance, and more confrontational methods are in evidence. In 2013, two Canadian scientists created a hitchhiking automaton dubbed hitch-BOT. HitchBOT could not move itself; rather, programmed with a rudimentary vocabulary and LED smiley face, it relied on friendly humans to help carry it to its next destination. The robot's design, manufactured out of scrap heap items— "a plastic bucket for a body, pool noodle arms and legs, and matching rubber gloves and boots"—was an effort to charm: "The low-tech look of it was intended to signal approachability rather than suggesting a complex high-end gadget," explained creators Frauke Zeller and David Harris Smith.[84] HitchBOT successfully trekked across Canada, was invited into homes and photographed at meals, and amassed a substantial social media following. Yet hitchBOT's inventors weren't simply staging a heartwarming bit of participatory art, although they boasted of their creation's status as the "robot in residence" at a number of museums. Their experiment had a serious utilitarian aim: in their words, "discovering how to optimally integrate human and robotic labor." And further, they argued that their project's success demonstrated the wide-ranging potential of robots in the workplace: "Robots aren't just an opportunity to make the office more efficient. Robots offer the chance to harness human creativity and to direct human attention."[85] The team made plans for hitchBOT to attempt to cross the United States, starting on the East Coast and ending up at the heart of everything tech, San Francisco.

HitchBOT made it as far as Philadelphia, where it was dismembered by unknown assailants two weeks after its American sojourn began. The scientists, who quickly absolved the City of Brotherly Love for any special culpability, made arrangements for hitchBOT's remains to be returned to Canada; its head was never found.[86] For an experiment to see whether robots could trust humans, it would seem an emphatic answer was provided on the sweltering summer streets of Philly.

If hitchBOT was a cartoonish vanguard for what *Financial Times* columnist Martin Wolf calls "the Rise of the Robots," then his assailants in Philadelphia also represent a kind of vanguard: a swift and forceful effort to sabotage the increasing proliferation of automatons in our lives.[87] In San Francisco, security robots hired to harass the homeless have been repeatedly assaulted (with one, in a testament to the boundless creativity of the masses, coated in barbeque sauce).[88] In Arizona, a testing ground for self-driving cars, AI-operated vehicles have met pitched resistance: residents have slashed tires, hurled rocks, flashed guns, and repeatedly attempted to run the cars off the road. For the Arizonans, the motive is self-preservation: in March of 2018, a driverless Uber struck and killed a woman in Tempe as she crossed the road.[89]

When robots enter the workplace, the antipathy is just as great. Researcher Matt Beane notes that when hospitals began to replace delivery workers with robots, workers began to sabotage the devices:

This took more violent forms—kicking them, hitting them with a baseball bat, stabbing their "faces" with pens, shoving, and punching. But much of this sabotage was more passive—hiding the robots in the basement, moving them outside their preplanned routes, obscuring sensors, walking slowly in front of them, and most of all, minimizing usage.

Beane dismisses the workers' actions as pointless: cutesy gizmos don't represent a true technological threat to livelihoods. But the sabotage is an emergent practice of machine-breaking that could develop into more concentrated workplace struggles. Beane notes that the attacks occurred amid tense negotiations for fairer work and pay.[90]

Inside the Amazon warehouses, where "full automation" is repeatedly shown to be a dream deferred,[91] workers direct their ire toward their robotic accessories. "We're human, not robots" has become a rallying cry for more humane, and less automated, working conditions. Other Amazon workers phrase their difficulties as a struggle against machines. "You have to beat the machine," said one temp worker at an Amazon fulfillment center. "It's like a nightmare, all these machines telling you your rate is down." When workers move too slowly, accruing more than three automated warnings, they are summarily canned, with managers hiding behind the technology. "Oh, we didn't fire you, the machine fired you because you are lower than the rate," explained warehouse temp worker Faizal Dualeh.[92]

And yet, on the floors of Amazon's logistical nodes, where industrial capitalism and surveillance capitalism seamlessly integrate into systems of domination that would make even Fred Taylor blush, workers find means of fighting back. Journalist Sam Adler-Bell documents Amazon workers' "weapons of the weak," methods they use to subvert Amazon's "regime of total surveillance and bodily control":

The warehouse workers I encountered play games, against themselves or their coworkers. They cheat to artificially boost their productivity numbers. They pass these tricks around in coded language. They use their scanners to find erroneously underpriced items and buy them in bulk. (Some steal outright.) They play (usually harmless) pranks on overbearing managers. And almost all of them skirt safety rules to move faster.[93]

While Adler-Bell is cautious about the efficacy of such tactics, he believes they show potential to spread: "Small acts—especially those that involve some sort of coordinated deception—may awaken a willingness to defy that eventually enables larger, more decisive acts." His conversations with Amazon workers broach the questions: What kinds of large, decisive acts might turn the tide against the machines and the massive companies behind them? How might we restore autonomy to our jobs and daily lives?

Conclusion

As I have documented in the preceding chapters, workers' movements of the past two centuries often had a Luddish bent: they understood new machines as weapons wielded against them in their struggles for a better life, and treated them as such. Intellectuals on both sides of the class struggle often characterized this perspective as shortsightedness, or downright irrationality. In spite of their political commitments to the working class, Marxist theoreticians often saw the capitalist development of technology as the means for creating both abundance and leisure, which would be realized once the masses finally took the reins of government and industry. These arguments continue to be made today: to take two examples, Leigh Phillips and Michal Rozworski's *People's Republic of Walmart* sees the discount retailer as the anticipation of socialist logistics, and Aaron Bastani's *Fully Automated Luxury Communism* devotes itself to speculative technologies like driverless cars and asteroid mining, with a "communist" coda at the end.[1] Both works self-consciously pitch themselves as restoring faith in a progressive, but politically neutral, technological telos, against a left politics that is small scale and "primitivist."

It is my contention, supported by the history of thought and action in the preceding pages, that the radical left can and should put forth a decelerationist politics: a politics of slowing down change, undermining technological progress, and limiting capital's rapacity, while developing organization and cultivating militancy. Letting Walmart or Amazon swallow the globe not only entrenches exploitative models of production and distribution; it channels resources to reactionary billionaires who use their wealth to further undermine the relative position of workers by funding conservative causes like tax cuts, school privatization, and opposition to gay marriage.[2] Letting technology take its course will lead not to egalitarian outcomes, but authoritarian ones, as the ultra-wealthy expend their resources on shielding themselves from any accountability to the rest of us: postapocalyptic bunkers, militarized yachts, private islands, and even escapes to outer space.[3]

Decelerationist politics is not the same as the "slow lifestyle" politics popular among segments of the better-off: "ways of being," as Carl Honoré puts it in the movement's manifesto, *In Praise of Slowness*, that emphasize "calm, careful, receptive, still, intuitive, unhurried, patient, reflective, quality-over-quantity."[4] As pleasing as slow aesthetics might be, I am not content to ground my argument in claims that a particular pace of life is "a more natural, human" one,[5] nor do I seek, as Honoré does, to give the capitalist system "a human face."[6] The argument for deceleration is not based on satisfying nature, human or otherwise, but in recognizing the challenges facing strategies for organizing the working class. The constant churn of recomposition and reorganization, what media scholar Nick Dyer-Witheford calls "the digital vortex" of contemporary capitalism, scarcely gives workers time to get back on their feet, let alone fight.[7] Decelerationism is not a withdrawal to a slower pace of life, but the manifestation of an antagonism toward the progress of elites at the expense of the rest of us. It is Walter Benjamin's emergency brake. It is a wrench in the gears.

This is to say, my argument is not based on lifestyle, or even ethics; it is based on politics. One of the biggest challenges facing the weak and fragmented left is how to compose ourselves as a class—how to organize diverse sectors of people to mobilize for fundamental social change. This is due to changes in the technical composition of capital that create new challenges for worker politics: the erosion of stable jobs, the use of digital technology to proliferate work tasks, the introduction of the precarious on-demand economy, the reinvention of Taylorism, the massive financial and ideological power of tech companies. Through Luddism, we can challenge some of these forces, and, as workers in the nineteenth century did, begin to discover our common goals—and our common enemies.

In this way, Luddism is not simply opposition to new machines or technologies, but a set of concrete politics with a positive content. Luddism, inspired as it is by workers' struggles at the point of production, emphasizes *autonomy*: the freedom of conduct, ability to set standards, and the continuity and improvement of working conditions. For the Luddites specifically, new machines were an immediate threat, and so Luddism contains a critical perspective on technology that pays particular attention to technology's relationship to the labor process and working conditions. In other words, it views technology not as neutral but as a *site of struggle*. Luddism *rejects production for production's sake*: it is critical of "efficiency" as an end goal, as there are other values at stake in work. Luddism can *generalize*: it is not an individual moral stance, but a series of practices that can proliferate and build through collective action. Finally, Luddism is *antagonistic*: it sets itself against existing capitalist social relations, which can only end through struggle, not through factors like state reforms, the increasing superfluity of goods, or a better planned economy.

My argument for Luddism rests on the fact that Luddism is popular, and the principle that radical intellectuals are better off listening to what people are saying than attempting to lead their thoughts. Currently the people are practically unanimous: they want to decelerate. A Pew Research Center poll found that 85 percent of Americans favored the restriction of automation to only the most dangerous forms of work.[8] Majorities oppose algorithmic automation of judgement in parole cases, job applications, and financial assessment, even when they acknowledge that such technologies might be effective.[9] In spite of pop accelerationist efforts to reenchant us with technological progress, we do not live in techno-optimistic times.

Luddism is not only popular; it also might just work. Carl Benedikt Frey, the economist who sparked panic with his claim that 47 percent of jobs would evaporate by 2034, has recently acknowledged the Luddite wave. "There is nothing to ensure that technology will always be allowed to progress uninterrupted," he writes. "It is perfectly possible for automation to become a political target."[10] He notes a variety of Luddite policies from the left: Jeremy Corbyn's proposed robot tax, Moon Jae-in's reduction of tax incentives for robotics, and even France's "biblio-diversity" law that forbids free shipping on discounted books, to better preserve bookstores from competition with Amazon.[11] History is full of reforms against the worst tendencies of technological development such as these, which will be an important component of the coming deceleration.

One of the most promising developments at the moment is the surge in militant organizing within Silicon Valley, which continues the Luddite tendency incubated within hacker culture. For instance, Google employees successfully pressured the company to abandon the Pentagon's AI initiative, Project Maven. Actions included software engineers' defiance of their superiors by refusing to work on the project.[12] The victory inspired workers at Salesforce, Microsoft, and Amazon to organize against their companies furnishment of AI and data processing capabilities to US immigration enforcement authorities.[13] These struggles are led and consolidated by organizations like the Tech Workers Coalition that hearken back to the Vietnam War–era organizations Computer People for Peace and Science for the People, which sought to seed the scientific and engineering communities with militants opposed to war and capitalism. The hashtag #TechWontBuildIt has become a slogan for developers who reject working on harmful technologies, a new strategy of refusal. It is a capacious slogan: rather than fantasize about technological marvels, we can envision all the horrors workers might refuse to produce, and the creative methods they might employ to disrupt this work.

Engineers and programmers at tech companies have a privileged place in the workforce, as their in-demand skills make them difficult to fire, granting them more room to advocate for themselves against management. But workers organizing inside Big Tech have deliberately expanded into the more precarious sectors of these corporations, supporting actions to unionize cafeteria workers at Facebook and security staff across the Bay Area.[14] At Google, full-time employees agitated around the company's exploitative use of temporary workers, a remarkable show of solidarity that led the company to raise its minimum standards for pay and benefits.[15] We may be seeing the composition of forces within technology companies that push them into less destructive and exploitative directions.

Beyond the tech industry, Luddite politics could link up with a number of emerging critical intellectual and political struggles. Here, movements to address the environmental crisis loom especially large. In spite of a few prominent voices that claim that current production and consumption patterns can continue in carbon-neutral ways by deploying new technology, it is increasingly clear that fundamental changes to the economic system are necessary if we are to have any hope of avoiding catastrophic climate change.[16] Green Luddism could be an alternative to the dead ends of technological solutionism and back-to-nature primitivism: a search for slower, less intensive, less estranged, more social methods of meeting our needs. Alyssa Battistoni offers an exemplary sketch of "a low-carbon society oriented toward the flourishing of all" centered on care work: "teaching, gardening, cooking, and nursing," all low-emission activities, conveniently involving workers who are increasingly involved in workplace struggles.[17] And environmental historian Troy Vettese's ambitious call for "natural geo-engineering" looks to Cuba as a model for a fossil fuel–free and rewilded globe that would also raise living standards for the vast majority of earth's population.[18]

Here is where Luddism might articulate with interest in the politics of degrowth. Degrowth originates in a critique of modernist developmental schemes for the global South, which presumed that Third World nations were required to follow a development template matching that of the industrialized North. As economist Serge LaTouche puts it, "the idea of degrowth was, in a sense, born in the South, and more specifically in Africa."[19] The failure of development in the economic sense, coupled with resentment over its Eurocentric devaluation of local customs and knowledge, had led African intellectuals to seek other options. Aligned with these concerns, LaTouche notes, was a recognition of imminent ecological crisis: "The growth society was not just undesirable but unsustainable!"[20] Degrowth shares with Luddism an acknowledgement that liberation is not tied up with endless accumulation of capital, and, further, that well-being cannot be reduced to economic statistics. As environmental scientist Giorgios Kallis and his coresearchers describe it, "Degrowth is not only about downscaling energy and resource use, but also about an overall project of exiting economism, that is, decolonizing the social imaginary and liberating public debate from prevalent discourses couched in economic terms, privileging growth."[21] And degrowth is not primitivism: in LaTouche's formulation, it could mean a return to "a material output equivalent to that of 1960–70."[22]

There are still other points of resonance with this decelerationist schema. Take, for instance, the Maintainers, a research network that seeks to shift focus of technological discourse away from "innovation" toward the vital practices of care and repair of existing technological infrastructures. "While innovation—the social process of introducing new things—is important," state codirectors Andy Russell and Lee Vinsel, "most technologies around us are old, and for the smooth functioning of daily life, maintenance is more important."[23] Further, the Maintainers seek to elevate and advocate for "crucial individuals who keep society's systems running": plumbers, elevator repair workers, computer code bug-fixers, safety officers.[24] As media anthropologist Shannon Mattern notes, the Maintainers share many of the concerns of degrowth advocates—"the waste of planned obsolescence, the environmental effects of unsustainable supply chains, the devaluation of care work, the underfunding of maintenance, and so forth."[25] And while the Maintainers often couch their efforts in the language of the mundane and humble, what they call for is nothing short of a radical break with how we encounter technology. Rather than a disruptive innovation delivered from on high by powerful capitalists, they argue for fragile socio-technical infrastructures, imbricated in the rhythms of our everyday lives and in which we have a vital stake. It is a politics that emphasizes social reproduction, rather than production, and that values a slower and more democratic engagement with technology.[26]

The "right to repair" movement stands as a Luddish technological initiative in the interest of conservation-minded maintenance. Currently much of our digital technology is locked down by manufacturers, who claim exclusive rights to repair and refurbish the gadgets we have purchased. Apple guards access to cheap spare parts, gouging customers at its Genius Bar to the point where buying a replacement becomes the cheaper option—an obvious boon to Apple, and an obvious waste of resources. Even technologies not thought of as digital are subject to such controls. For example, proprietary software in new John Deere tractors comes with a license that requires the company to authorize the installation of any new parts. Says farmer Kevin Kenney,

You want to replace a transmission and you take it to an independent mechanic—he can put in the new transmission but the tractor can't drive out of the shop. Deere charges $230, plus $130 an hour for a technician to drive out and plug a connector into their USB port to authorize the part.[27]

In response, some farmers are hacking their software with cracks downloaded from Eastern European forums, in an effort to keep their equipment stable, open, and able to repair. It is pure Luddism in action, a refusal to submit to techno-capitalist demands to relinquish skill and autonomy, a ripping-open of the walled gardens of code.

The right to repair movement seeks to legitimate these practices through legal reform and has earned powerful political allies such as Massachusetts Senator Elizabeth Warren.[28] Other organizations work along grassroots lines. In the UK, the Restart Project seeks to restore our ability to fix and tinker with our devices as we see fit, rather than succumb to market imperatives that reward disposal and overproduction. Rather than simply save consumers time and money, Restart envisions its work as altering the relationship between technology and its users through training workshops:

> By bringing people together to share skills and gain the confidence to open up their stuff, we give people a hands-on way of making a difference, as well as a way to talk about the wider issue of what kind of products we want.[29]

To be sure, these contemporary projects are vibrant, diverse, and, in some sense, incommensurate. The same is true of many of the historical movements I've discussed in this book. Luddism manifests itself differently according to context. It is not a political program that various organizations and initiatives have signed on to in advance, but something more inchoate, a kind of diffuse sensibility that nevertheless constitutes a significant antagonism to the way that capitalism operates. And it can precipitate into concrete coalitions in unexpected ways.

Effective radical politics doesn't follow from an airtight plan constructed ahead of time with a specific revolutionary subject in mind. Even victorious revolutions are haphazard things, where disparate antagonisms build up, merge, and fragment. Louis Althusser, studying Lenin's analysis of the success of the Bolshevik Revolution, argued that it was not a case where the proletariat simply became sufficiently large and organized to overthrow the state. Rather, the revolution was a "ruptural unity": "an accumulation of 'circumstances' and 'currents' so that whatever their origin and sense (and many of them will necessarily be paradoxically foreign to the revolution in origin and sense, or even its 'direct opponents')."[30] As the cultural theorist Stuart Hall put it in his own reading of Althusser,

> The aim of a theoretically-informed political practice must surely be to bring about or construct the articulation between social or economic forces and those forms of politics and ideology which might lead them in practice to intervene in history in a progressive way.[31]

My hope is that recognizing Luddism at work in the office, on the shop floor, at school, and in the street aids the ambitions of contemporary radicals by giving anti-technology sentiment a historical depth, theoretical sophistication, and political relevance. We may discover each other through our myriad of antagonistic practices in their incredible diversity, connecting to other struggles against the concentrated power of capital and the state, pitched, in the words of Althusser, of "different origins, different sense, different levels and points of application."[32] To do so requires no preconstructed plan, no litmus tests of what is necessary in order to be properly political, authentically radical, or legitimately left. As Marx put it in a late letter to the Dutch socialist Ferdinand Domela

Nieuwenhuis, "The doctrinaire and necessarily fantastic anticipations of the programme of action for a revolution of the future only divert us from the struggle of the present."[33] Rather, the first step of organizing disparate grievances into a collective politics requires recognizing and recovering our own radical self-activity along with that of others. Even, and perhaps especially, when it involves breaking things at work.

Notes

Introduction

1 Kenneth Chang, "Jeff Bezos Unveils Blue Origin's Vision for Space, and a Moon Lander," *New York Times*, May 9, 2019, nytimes.com

2 Corey S. Powell, "Jeff Bezos foresees a trillion people living in millions of space colonies. Here's what he's doing to get the ball rolling," NBC News, May 15, 2019, nbcnews.com.

3 Ibid.

4 Tom McKay, "Elon Musk: A New Life Awaits You in the Off-World Colonies—for a Price," *Gizmodo*, January 17, 2020, gizmodo.com.

5 Elon Musk, "Making Life Multiplanetary," abridged transcript of presentation at the 68th International Astronomical Congress, September 28, 2017, spacex.com.

6 Mark Zuckerberg, "Bringing the World Closer Together," Facebook note, June 22, 2017, facebook.com.

7 Peter Thiel with Blake Masters, *Zero to One: Notes on Start-ups, or How to Build the Future* (New York: Crown Business, 2014), 5.

8 Ibid., 70.

9 Steven Pinker, *Enlightenment Now: The Case for Reason, Science, Humanism, and Progress* (New York: Viking, 2018), 40.

10 Ibid., 109.

11 Ibid., 118.

12 Catherine de Lange and Sherry Turkle, "We're Losing the Raw, Human Part of Being with Each Other," interview, *Guardian*, May 5, 2013, theguardian.com.

13 Tim Wu, *The Attention Merchants* (New York: Knopf, 2016), 343–4.

14 Martin Heidegger, "The Question Concerning Technology," in *Martin Heidegger: Basic Writings*, trans. W. Lovitt, ed. D.F. Krell, rev. ed. (London: Routledge, 1993), 311–41.

15 Jack Rear, "How to Give Yourself a Proper Digital Detox ... according to Google," *Telegraph*, February 8, 2019.

1. The Nights of King Ludd

1 FRAME WORK BILL, HL Deb 27 February 1812 vol 21 cc964-79, parliament.uk.

2 George Gordon Byron. *The Works of Lord Byron: Poetry: Vol. VII.* ed. E.H. Coleridge (London: John Murray, Albemarle Street, 1904), 42.

3 E.P. Thompson, *The Making of the English Working Class*, (New York: Vintage, 1966).

4 Jamillah Knowles, "'I'm Not a Luddite'—Andrew Keen Talks about His New Book *Digital Vertigo*," *NextWeb*, May 26, 2012, thenextweb.com.

5 See, respectively, Daniel W. Drezner, "Confessions of a Luddite professor," *Washington Post*, April 28, 2016, washingtonpost .com; Gareth D. Smith, "Confessions of a Luddite: My Eventual Acceptance of Technology in Performance," *Thinking about Music*, January 3, 2015, thinkingaboutmusic.com; Sanford Hess, "Confessions of a Closet Luddite," LinkedIn blog post, August 23, 2016, linkedin.com/pulse/confessions-closet-luddite-sanford-hess.

6 Thomas Pynchon, "Is It O.K. to Be a Luddite?," *New York Times*, October 28, 1984.

7 Chellis Glendenning, "Notes toward a Neo-Luddite Manifesto," *Utne Reader*, March/April 1990.

8 Kaczynski's manifestos were published by radical environmental group Earth First!, and he drew vocal support from anarcho-primitivist writer John Zerzan. See Kenneth B. Noble, "Prominent Anarchist Finds Unsought Ally in Serial Bomber," *New York Times*, May 7, 1995.

9 Jack Hunter, "Radical Kirk," *American Conservative*, June 16, 2011, theamericanconservative.com.

10 Marco Deseriis, *Improper Names: Collective Pseudonyms from the Luddites to Anonymous* (Minneapolis: University of Minnesota Press, 2015), 68.

11 Karl Marx, *Capital: A Critique of Political Economy*, vol. 1 (London: Penguin Books, [1867] 1992), 554.

12 "Albion's Dark Satanic Mill," *The Printshop Window* (blog), November 15, 2013, theprintshopwindow.com.

13 Andrew Ure, *Philosophy of Manufactures* (Ann Arbor: University of Michigan Press, [1835] 2007), 257.

14 Kirkpatrick Sale, *Rebels against the Future: The Luddites and Their War on the Industrial Revolution* (Boston: Addison-Wesley, 1996), 18.

15 Thompson, *English Working Class*, 12–13.

16 Sale, *Rebels against the Future*, 3.

17 Ibid., 68.

18 Eric J. Hobsbawm, "The Machine Breakers," *Past and Present* 1 (February 1952), 58.

19 Kevin Binfield, *Writings of the Luddites* (Baltimore: Johns Hopkins University Press, 2015), 90.

20 Hobsbawm, "Machine Breakers," 60.

21 Ibid., 61.

22 See Steven Wright, *Storming Heaven*, 107.

23 "General Introduction to Zerowork," *Zerowork* 1 (1975).

24 Salar Mohandesi, "Class Consciousness or Class Composition?," *Science and Society* 77:1 (January 2013), 79–80.

25 Peter Linebaugh, *Ned Ludd and Queen Mab: Machine-Breaking, Romanticism, and the Several Commons of 1811–12*, pamphlet (Oakland: PM Press, 2012), 10.

26 Ibid., 24.

27 Eugene D. Genovese, *The Political Economy of Slavery* (Middletown: Wesleyan University Press, 1989), 55.

28 Linebaugh, *Ned Ludd*, 23.

29 Ure, *Philosophy of Manufactures*, 280.

30 David Ricardo, *On the Principles of Political Economy and Taxation* (London: John Murray, 1817).

31 Karl Marx and Friedrich Engels, *The Communist Manifesto* (London: Workers' Educational Association, 1848).

32 Karl Marx, *A Contribution to the Critique of Political Economy* (Moscow: Progress Publishers, [1859] 1967).

33 Donald MacKenzie, "Marx and the Machine." *Technology and Culture*, 25:3 (July, 1984), pp 476–8.

34 Karl Marx, *Grundrisse* (New York: Penguin, [1939] 2005), 693.

35 Ibid.
36 Ibid., 694.
37 Maurizio Lazzarato, "Immaterial Labor" in *Radical Thought in Italy: A Potential Politics*, ed. Paolo Virno and Michael Hardt (Minneapolis, MN: University of Minnesota Press, 1996) 133–50.
38 Michael Hardt and Antonio Negri, *Empire* (Cambridge, MA: Harvard University Press, 2000), 294.
39 Paul Mason, *Postcapitalism: A Guide to Our Future* (New York: Macmillan, 2016); Aaron Bastani, "What Would a Populist Corbyn Look Like?" *Open Democracy*, December 22, 2016, opendemocracy.net. For an extensive critique of Mason, see Frederick H. Pitts, "Review of Paul Mason—*Postcapitalism: A Guide to Our Future*," *Marx and Philosophy Review of Books*, September 4, 2015, marxandphilosophy.org.uk.
40 Michael Heinrich, "The 'Fragment on Machines': A Marxian Misconception in the Grundrisse and its Overcoming in Capital," in *In Marx's Laboratory: Critical Interpretations of the Grundrisse*, eds. Riccardo Bellofiore, Guido Starosta, and Peter D. Thomas (Chicago: Haymarket, 2014).
41 Marx and Engels, *Capital*, 562, 563.
42 The Penguin edition of *Capital* includes it as an appendix.
43 Ibid., 1025.
44 Ibid., 1026.
45 Ibid., 1035.
46 Ibid., 990.
47 Nicolas Thoburn, *Deleuze, Marx, and Politics* (London: Routledge, 2003), 78.
48 Marx and Engels, *Capital*, 1037, 1035.
49 "A History of Subsumption," *Endnotes* 2 (2010), 131.
50 Patrick Murray, "The Social and Material Transformation of Production by Capital: Formal and Real Subsumption in Capital, Volume I," in *The Constitution of Capital*, eds. Riccardo Bellofiore and Nicola Taylor (New York: Palgrave Macmillan, 2004), 252.
51 Marx and Engels, *Capital*, 1019.
52 Jan Breman, *Footloose Labour: Working in India's Informal Economy* (Cambridge, UK: Cambridge University Press, 1996). On artisanal mining, see for example "Interconnected Supply Chains: A Comprehensive Look at Due Diligence Challenges and

Opportunities Sourcing Cobalt and Copper from the Democratic Republic of the Congo," OECD Working Paper (Paris: OECD, 2019).

53 Karl Marx, *The Poverty of Philosophy* (New York: International Publishers, [1847] 1992), 209.
54 Marx and Engels, *Capital*, 554–5.
55 Karl Marx and Friedrich Engels, *The German Ideology* (New York: International Publishers, [1932] 1970).
56 Michelle Perrot, "On the Formation of the French Working Class," in *Working-Class Formation: Nineteenth-Century Patterns in Western Europe and the United States*, eds. Ira Katznelson and Aristide R. Zolberg (Princeton: Princeton University Press, 1987), 72–3.
57 Ibid., 74.
58 Ibid., 82.
59 Ibid., 82–9.
60 Ibid., 85.
61 Clive Wilmer, "Introduction," in William Morris, *News from Nowhere and Other Writings* (New York: Penguin [1890], 1994), xxii.
62 Ibid., 289.
63 Ibid., 295.
64 Ibid., 296.
65 Ibid., 302.
66 Ibid., 304.
67 Ibid., 354.
68 Marx and Engels, *The Communist Manifesto*.
69 Ibid.
70 Morris, *News from Nowhere*, 355.

2. Tinkerers, Taylors, Soldiers, Wobs

1 Hugh G.J. Aitken, *Taylorism at Watertown Arsenal: Scientific Management in Action 1908–1915* (Cambridge, MA: Harvard University Press, 1960), 8–9.
2 Ibid, 50.
3 Robert Kanigel, "Taylor-Made: How the World's First Efficiency Expert Refashioned Modern Life in His Image," *Sciences* 37:3 (May/June 1997), 18–23.

4 Harry Braverman, *Labor and Monopoly Capital* (New York: Monthly Review, 1974), 62.

5 Quoted in Charles Wrege and Anne Marie Stotka, "Cooke Creates a Classic: The Story Behind F.W. Taylor's Principles of Scientific Management," *Academy of Management Review* 3:4 (October 1978), 736.

6 James Hoopes, *False Prophets: The Gurus Who Created Modern Management and Why Their Ideas Are Bad for Business Today* (New York: Basic Books, 2003); Jill Lepore, "Not So Fast," *New Yorker*, October 5, 2009.

7 Quoted in David Stark, "Class Struggle and the Transformation of the Labor Process: A Relational Approach," *Theory and Society* 9:1 (January 1980), 105.

8 Bryan Palmer, "Class, Conception, and Conflict: The Thrust for Efficiency, Managerial Views of Labor, and the Working Class Rebellion, 1903–22," *Review of Radical Political Economics* 7:2 (July 1975), 36.

9 Adam Smith, *The Wealth of Nations* (New York: The Modern Library, [1776] 2000), 840.

10 Frederick W. Taylor, *The Principles of Scientific Management* (New York and London: Harper & Brothers, [1911] 1913).

11 David R. Roediger and Elizabeth D. Esch, *The Production of Difference: Race and the Management of Labor in US History* (New York: Oxford University Press, 2012), 148.

12 Taylor, *Scientific Management*.

13 *Testimony of Frederick W. Taylor before Special Committee of the US House of Representatives to Investigate the Taylor and Other Systems of Shop Management*, January 1912 (Washington, DC: Government Printing Office, 1912), 1879.

14 Robert F. Hoxie, "Why Organized Labor Opposes Scientific Management," *Quarterly Journal of Economics* 31:1 (November 1916), 62–85.

15 Aitken, *Taylorism at Watertown Arsenal*, 45.

16 Karl Kautsky, *The Class Struggle* (Chicago: Charles H. Kerr & Co., [1892] 1910).

17 Geoff Eley, *Forging Democracy: The History of the Left in Europe, 1850–2000* (New York: Oxford University Press, 2002), 110.

18 Rosa Luxemburg, *Social Reform or Revolution?* (New York: Pathfinder, [1899] 1973).

19 Lucio Colletti, *From Rousseau to Lenin* (New York: New York University Press, 1975), 54.

20 Ibid., 65.

21 This entire technologically determinist version of the transition from capitalism to socialism, including its attendant mistake of viewing "forces of production" strictly in terms of capitalist production technologies, was revived in the 1970s by G.A. Cohen and the "analytic Marxism" school. See Sayer's *The Violence of Abstraction* (1987) for a critique that draws from many of the same arguments as Colletti.

22 Karl Kautsky, "Constituent Assembly and Soviet," in *The Dictatorship of the Proletariat* (Manchester, UK: National Labour Press, [1918] 1919), chapter 6.

23 Eley, *Forging Democracy*, 126.

24 Dick Geary, *Karl Kautsky* (Manchester, UK: Manchester University Press, 1987), 91.

25 Bhaskar Sunkara, *The Socialist Manifesto: The Case for Radical Politics in an Age of Extreme Inequality* (New York: Basic Books, 2017), 118.

26 Mike Davis, "The Stopwatch and the Wooden Shoe," *Radical America* (January/February 1975), 74.

27 Walker C. Smith, *Sabotage: Its History, Philosophy, and Function* (Chicago: Black Swan Press, 1913).

28 Ibid.

29 Elizabeth Gurley Flynn, *Sabotage* (Cleveland: IWW Publishing Bureau, 1916).

30 Thorstein Veblen, *On the Nature and Uses of Sabotage*, (New York: Dial Press, 1919), 5.

31 See Graham Cassano, "Stylistic Sabotage and Thorstein Veblen's Scientific Irony," *Journal of Economic Issues* 39:3 (September 2005), 741–64.

32 John F. Henry, "Fred Lee, the Industrial Workers of the World, and Heterodox Economics," *Review of Radical Political Economics* 49:1, (March 2017), 148–52.

33 Sidney Plotkin and Rick Tilman, *The Political Ideas of Thorstein Veblen* (New Haven: Yale University Press, 2011), 214n52.

34 Veblen, *Sabotage*, 45.

35 Beverly H. Burris, *Technocracy at Work* (New York: SUNY Press, 1993), 28–9.

36 "Technocracy: A Bloodless Revolution," *Technocrat's Magazine*, 1933, 4–5.
37 Ibid., 6.
38 Ibid, 13.
39 David F. Noble, *America By Design: Science, Technology, and the Rise of Corporate Capitalism* (New York: Oxford University Press, 1979), 63.
40 Andor Wiener, "Technocracy or Industrial Unionism," trans. Ildiko Sipos (Cleveland: Bérmunkás, 1933).
41 Alexei Kojevnikov, "The Phenomenon of Soviet Science," *Osiris*, 2nd series, 23 (2008), 116.
42 Nikolai Bukharin, *The Theory of Historical Materialism: A Popular Textbook of Marxist Sociology* (Moscow: International Publishers, 1921).
43 Georg Lukács, "Technology and Social Relations," *New Left Review* 39 (September/October 1966).
44 Vladimir Ilyich Lenin, "The Taylor System: Man's Enslavement by the Machine," in *Lenin Collected Works*, vol. 20, trans. Bernard Isaacs and Joe Fineburg (Moscow: Progress Publishers, [1914] 1972).
45 Vladimir Ilyich Lenin, "The Immediate Tasks of the Soviet Government," in *Lenin Collected Works*, vol. 27, trans. Clemens Dutt, ed. Robert Daglish (Moscow: Progress Publishers, [1918] 1972).
46 Ibid.
47 Alexander Bogdanov, "Socially Organised Society: Socialist Society," *A Short Course of Economic Science*, rev. ed., trans. Joe Fineburg (London: Communist Party of Great Britain, [1919] 1925), chapter 10.
48 Zenovia A. Sochor, "Soviet Taylorism Revisited," *Soviet Studies* 33:2 (1981), 248–9.
49 Richard Stites, *Revolutionary Dreams: Utopian Vision and Experimental Life in the Russian Revolution* (New York: Oxford University Press, 1991), 152.
50 Quoted in Stites, *Revolutionary Dreams*, 151.
51 Quoted in Kendall E. Bailes, "Alexei Gastev and the Soviet Controversy over Taylorism, 1918–24," *Soviet Studies* 29:3 (July 1977), 378.
52 Paul Avrich, *Kronstadt, 1921* (Princeton: Princeton University Press, 1970), 29.
53 Stites, *Revolutionary Dreams*, 164.

54 Stephen Kotkin, *Magnetic Mountain: Stalinism as a Civilization* (Berkeley: University of California Press, 1995), 32.
55 Ibid., 38.
56 Louis Althusser, "On the Primacy of the Relations of Production over the Productive Forces," in *On the Reproduction of Capitalism: Ideology and Ideological State Apparatuses* (London and New York: Verso, 2014), 215.
57 Kotkin, *Magnetic Mountain*, 45.
58 Jeffrey Rossman, *Worker Resistance under Stalin: Class and Revolution on the Shop Floor* (Cambridge, MA: Harvard University Press, 2005), 6.
59 Ibid., 150.
60 Ibid., 125.
61 Walter Benjamin, *The Arcades Project* (Cambridge, MA: Harvard University Press, 1999), 460.
62 Walter Benjamin, "The Work of Art in the Age of Mechanical Reproduction," in *Illuminations: Essays and Reflections*, ed. Hannah Arendt, trans. Harry Zohn (Boston: Houghton Mifflin Harcourt, 1968).
63 Ibid.
64 Walter Benjamin, "Author as Producer," *Understanding Brecht* (London and New York: Verso, [1966] 1998), 95.
65 Gary D. Rhodes, *The Perils of Moviegoing in America: 1896–1950* (New York: Continuum, 2012), 109–10.
66 Walter Benjamin, "Theses on the Philosophy of History" (1942), in *Illuminations*.
67 Michael Löwy, *Fire Alarm: Reading Walter Benjamin's "On the Concept of History"* (London and New York: Verso, 2016), 70.
68 Mary Nolan, *Visions of Modernity: American Business and the Modernization of Germany* (Oxford: Oxford University Press, 1994), 25.
69 Ibid., 41.
70 Ibid., 82.
71 Ibid., 168.
72 Ibid., 231.
73 Walter Benjamin, "On the Concept of History," in *Selected Writings*, vol. 4, *1938–1940*, ed. Howard Eiland and Michael W. Jennings, trans. Edmund Jephcott et al. (Cambridge, MA: Belknap, [2003]), 392.

74 Walter Benjamin, "Paralipomena to 'On the Concept of History,' in *Selected Writings*, vol. 4, *1938–1940*, ed. Howard Eiland and Michael W. Jennings, trans. Edmund Jephcott et al. (Cambridge, MA: Belknap, [2003]), 402.

75 Benjamin, "On the Concept of History," 390.

76 Löwy, *Fire Alarm*, 95.

3. Against Automation

1 David Hounsell, "Ford Automates: Technology and Organization in Theory and Practice," *Business and Economic History* Vol. 24, No. 1, papers presented at the forty-first annual meeting of the Business History Conference (Fall 1995), 69.

2 David Hounsell, "Planning and Executing 'Automation' at Ford Motor Company, 1945–1965: The Cleveland Engine Plant and its Consequences," in *Fordism Transformed: The Development of Production Methods in the Automobile Industry*, ed. Haruhito Shiomi and Kazuo Wada (Oxford University Press, 1996), 70.

3 Nelson Lichtenstein, *The Most Dangerous Man In Detroit: Walter Reuther And The Fate Of American Labor* (New York: Basic Books, 1995), 290.

4 Carl Benedikt Frey and Michael A. Osborne, "The Future of Employment: How Susceptible Are Jobs to Computerization," Oxford Martin School Working Paper, September 2013.

5 Nick Srnicek and Alex Williams, *Inventing the Future: Postcapitalism and a World without Work* (London and New York: Verso, 2015), 253.

6 Peter Frase, *Four Futures: Life after Capitalism* (London and New York: Verso, 2016), 42.

7 Aaron Bastani, *Fully Automated Luxury Communism* (London and New York: Verso, 2019), 189.

8 David H. Autor, "Why Are There Still So Many Jobs? The History and Future of Workplace Automation," *Journal of Economic Perspectives* 29:3 (2015), 3–30.

9 Ibid., 11.

10 Jefferson Graham, "Flippy the burger-flipping robot is on a break already," *USAToday*, March 9, 2018.

11 See Harry Cleaver, *Reading Capital Politically* (San Francisco: AK Press, 2000), 115–17.

12 "Automation," Oral Answers to Questions, House of Commons Debate, May 8, 1959, available at api.parliament.uk.

13 Ibid.

14 Cornelius Castoriadis, *Political and Social Writings*, vol. 2, trans. and ed. David Ames (Minneapolis: University of Minnesota Press, 1988), 35.

15 David F. Noble, *Forces of Production: A Social History of Industrial Production* (New York: Oxford University Press, 1986), 5.

16 Ibid., 83–4.

17 Ibid., 22–3.

18 Peter Galison, "The Ontology of the Enemy: Norbert Wiener and the Cybernetic Vision," *Critical Inquiry* 21:1 (Autumn 1994), 233.

19 Norbert Wiener, *Cybernetics; or, Control and Communication in the Animal and the Machine* (Cambridge, MA: MIT Press, 1965), 37.

20 Norbert Wiener, *The Human Use of Human Beings: Cybernetics and Society* (Boston: Houghton Mifflin, 1950), 181.

21 Norbert Weiner, letter to UAW President Walter Reuther, August 13, 1949, available at libcom.org.

22 Quoted in Peter Hudis, "Workers as Reason: The Development of a New Relation of Worker and Intellectual in American Marxist Humanism," *Historical Materialism* 11:4 (January 2003), 270.

23 Quoted in Noble, *Forces of Production*, 249.

24 Paul Romano and Ria Stone, *The American Worker* (Detroit: Bewick, [1947] 1972), available at libcom.org.

25 Hudis, "Workers as Reason," 273.

26 C.L.R. James and Grace C. Lee, *Facing Reality* (Correspondence Publishing, 1958), 26–7.

27 Raya Dunayevskaya, *Marxism and Freedom: From 1776 until Today* (London: Pluto, 1975), 3.

28 Ibid., 264–5.

29 Ibid., 269.

30 Ibid., 270.

31 See Kevin B. Anderson, "Introduction" in *The Dunayevskaya-Marcuse-Fromm Correspondence 1954-1978*, eds. Kevin B. Anderson and Russell Rockwell (Lanham: Lexington Books, 2012).

32 Charles Denby, "Workers Battle Automation," *News and Letters*, November 1960, 29.

33 Ibid., 13.

34 Ibid., 46.

35 Ibid., 47.
36 Herbert Marcuse, *One-Dimensional Man: Studies in the Ideology of Advanced Industrial Society* (Boston: Beacon, 1964), 33.
37 Ibid., 40.
38 Anderson and Rockwell, *Dunayevskaya-Marcuse-Fromm Correspondence*, 227.
39 Ibid., 228.
40 Denby, "Workers Battle Automation," 44.
41 Marc Levinson, *The Box: How the Shipping Container Made the World Smaller and the World Economy Bigger* (Princeton, Princeton University Press, 2006), 24–6.
42 Stan Weir, *Singlejack Solidarity* (Minneapolis: University of Minnesota Press 2004), 95.
43 E.P. Thompson, *The Making of the English Working Class* (New York: Pantheon, 1963), 291.
44 Weir, *Singlejack Solidarity*, 104.
45 Marco d'Eramo, "Dock Life," *New Left Review* 96 (November/December 2015), 89.
46 Weir, *Singlejack Solidarity*, 48.
47 Ibid., 49.
48 Ibid., 94–5.
49 Levinson, *The Box*, 100.
50 Weird, *Singlejack Solidarity*, 45.
51 Levinson, *The Box*, 184.
52 Levinson, *The Box*, 186–8.
53 Martin Glaberman, "'Be His Payment High or Low': The American Working Class in the Sixties," *International Socialism* 21 (Summer 1965), 18–23.
54 Ibid., 23.
55 Steven Greenhouse, "Union Dispute, Turning Violent, Spreads and Idles Ports," *New York Times*, September 8, 2011, nytimes.com.
56 Aaron Corvin, "United Grain Corp. Accuses ILWU of Sabotage, Locks Out Workers," *Daily Columbian*, February 26, 2013.
57 Martin Luther King Jr., quoted in Marcus D. Pohlmann, *African American Political Thought: Capitalism vs. Collectivism, 1945 to the Present* (New York: Taylor & Francis, 2003), 77.
58 A.B. Spellman, "Interview with Malcolm X," *Monthly Review* 16:1 (May 1964).
59 Ad Hoc Committee on the Triple Revolution, *The Triple Revolution*, pamphlet, 1964.

60 Ibid.
61 John Pomfret, "Guaranteed Income Asked for All, Employed or Not," *New York Times*, March 23, 1964.
62 Daniel Bell, "The Bogey of Automation," *New York Review of Books*, August 26, 1965.
63 Herbert R. Northrup, "Equal Opportunity and Equal Pay," in *The Negro and Equal Opportunity*, eds. H.R. Northrup and Richard L. Rowan (Ann Arbor: Bureau of Industrial Relations, 1965) 85–107.
64 Paul M. Sweezy and Paul A. Baran, *Monopoly Capital: An Essay on the American Economic and Social Order* (New York: Monthly Review, 1966), 267.
65 Ibid., 268.
66 Ernest Mandel, "Where Is America Going?," *New Left Review* 54 (March/April 1969).
67 Robert L. Allen, *Black Awakening in Capitalist America* (Trenton: Africa World Press, [1969] 1990), 3.
68 Sidney Willhelm, *Who Needs the Negro?* (New York: Schenkman, 1970), 3.
69 Ibid., 136.
70 Ibid, 165.
71 Ibid.
72 Eldridge Cleaver, *On the Ideology of the Black Panther Party* (Oakland: Black Panther Party, 1969), 7.
73 Ibid., 9.
74 Huey Newton, "Revolutionary Intercommunalism," lecture, Boston College, November 18, 1970, available at libcom.org.
75 Dan Georgakas and Marvin Surkin, *Detroit: I Do Mind Dying* (New York: South End Press, 1998), 102.
76 Clayborne Carson and David Malcolm Carson, "Black Panther Party," in *Encyclopedia of the American Left*, edited by Mari Jo Buhle et al. (New York: Garland Publishing, 1990).
77 Cynthia Cockburn, "Caught in the Wheels: The High Cost of Being a Female Cog in the Male Machinery of Engineering," in *The Social Shaping of Technology*, eds. Donald MacKenzie and Judith Wajcman (Buckingham, UK: Open University Press, 1999), 56.
78 Venus Green, *Race on the Line: Gender, Labor, and Technology in the Bell System, 1880–1980* (Durham: Duke University Press, 2001), 91.

79 Ibid., 187.

80 Ibid., 128.

81 Frank B. Gilbreth Jr. and Ernestine Gilbreth Carey, *Cheaper by the Dozen* (New York: Perennial Classics, 2002).

82 Tilla Siegel and Nicholas Levis, "It's Only Rational: An Essay on the Logic of Social Rationalization," *International Journal of Political Economy* 24:4 (Winter 1994–95), 35–70.

83 Antonio Gramsci, *Prison Notebooks*, vol. 1, ed. Joseph Buttigieg (New York: Columbia University Press, 1992) 286.

84 Selma James and Mariarosa Dalla Costa, *The Power of Women and the Subversion of the Community* (Bristol, UK: Falling Wall Press, 1975).

85 Ruth Cowan, *More Work For Mother: The Ironies of Household Technology from the Open Hearth to the Microwave* (New York: Basic Books, 1983), 44.

86 Ibid., 47.

87 Ibid., 197.

88 Firestone is an acknowledged precursor to the cyborg feminism of Donna Haraway, and with her inclusion in the anthology *#Accelerate: The Accelerationist Reader* (Falmouth, UK: Urbanomic, 2014), she has been canonized as a proto-accelerationist thinker. See Debora Halbert, "Shulamith Firestone," *Information, Communication and Society* 7:1 (2007), 115–35.

89 Shulamith Firestone, *The Dialectic of Sex: The Case for Feminist Revolution* (New York: Bantam Books, 1970), 8.

90 Ibid., 10–11.

91 Ibid., 31.

92 Ibid., 196.

93 Donna Haraway, *A Cyborg Manifesto, Socialist Review* 80 (1985), 65–108.

94 Firestone, *Dialectic of Sex*, 201.

95 FINRRAGE, "Resolution and Comilla Declaration," in *Feminist Manifestos: A Global Documentary Reader*, ed. Penny A. Weiss (New York: New York University Press, 2018), 307.

96 Sophie Lewis, "Defending Intimacy against What? Limits of Antisurrogacy Feminisms," *Signs: Journal of Women in Culture and Society* 43:1 (2017), 98.

97 Judy Wajcman, *Feminism Confronts Technology* (University Park: Pennsylvania State University Press, 1991), 62.

98 FINRRAGE, "Resolution," 309.

4. High-Tech Luddism

1 Steven Lubar, "'Do Not Fold, Spindle or Mutilate': A Cultural History of the Punch Card," *Journal of American Culture* 15:4 (Winter 1992), 46.

2 Ibid., 48.

3 Donald Fisher Harrison, "Computers, Electronic Data, and the Vietnam War," *Archavia* 26 (Summer 1988), 18.

4 Address by General W.C. Westmoreland to the Association of the US Army, US Senate Congressional Record, October 16, 1969, 30348.

5 Ian G.R. Shaw, "Scorched Atmospheres: The Violent Geographies of the Vietnam War and the Rise of Drone Warfare," *Annals of the American Association of Geographers* 106:3 (2016), 695.

6 Science and Engineers for Social and Political Action, *Science against the People* (Berkeley: SESPA, 1972), 8.

7 Paul Dickson, *The Electronic Battlefield* (Takoma Park: FoxAcre Press, 2012), 85.

8 See the noteworthy slideshow put together by the Quaker anti-war group National Action/Research on the Military Industrial Complex (NARMIC), available as of this writing on YouTube: "Automated Air War," uploaded by American Friends Service Committee, 30 mins. 52 secs., youtube.com.

9 Immanuel Wallerstein and Paul Starr, eds., *University Crisis Reader*, vol. 2 (New York: Vintage, 1971), 240–1.

10 Jonathan Croyle, "Throwback Thursday: Student Protests Close Syracuse University in 1970," *Post-Standard* (Syracuse), May 5, 2016, syracuse.com.

11 "Vietnam War Protests at the University of Wisconsin-Milwaukee: The Student Strike and Later Protests, 1970–1972," University of Wisconsin–Milwaukee Libraries, guides.library.uwm.edu.

12 James Barron, "The Mathematicians Who Ended the Kidnapping of an NYU Computer," *New York Times*, December 6, 2015, nytimes.com.

13 US Senate Congressional Record, February 21, 1972, 4786–7.

14 See Fred Turner's masterful *From Counterculture to Cyberculture* (Chicago: University of Chicago Press, 2006) for a detailed historical account of this transition, as well as Richard Barbrook and Andy Cameron's essay "The Californian Ideology," *Science as Culture* 6:1 (1996), 44–72.

15 Harry Braverman, *Labor and Monopoly Capital: The Degradation of Work in the Twentieth* Century (New York: Monthly Review, 1974), 334.
16 Quoted in Shoshana Zuboff, *In the Age of the Smart Machine: The Future of Work and Power* (New York: Basic Books, 1989), 120.
17 Quoted in Braverman, *Labor and Monopoly Capital*, 231–2.
18 Zuboff, *In the Age of the Smart Machine*, 7.
19 Ibid., 10.
20 Ibid., 291.
21 Ibid., 347.
22 Ibid., 352–3.
23 Chris Carlsson and Adam Cornford, "Talking Heads," in *Bad Attitude: The Processed World Anthology* (London and New York: Verso, 1990), 7.
24 Ibid., 13.
25 Steven Wright, "Beyond a Bad Attitude? Information Workers and Their Prospects through the Pages of *Processed World*," *Journal of Information Ethics* 20:2 (2011).
26 "J.M.," in *Bad Attitude*, 43.
27 Gidget Digit, "Sabotage: The Ultimate Video Game," in *Bad Attitude*, 59.
28 "D.E.," in *Bad Attitude*, 31.
29 Ibid.
30 Zuboff, "Sabotage," 63.
31 Zuboff, "Sabotage," 64.
32 Tom Athanisou, "New Information Technology: For What?," *Processed World* 1 (April 1981).
33 Holz, "Letters," *Processed World* 9, 7–8
34 Digit, "Sabotage, 65.
35 Important contributions to this debate include Gabriella Coleman and Adam Golub, "Hacker Practice: Moral Genres and the Cultural Articulation of Liberalism," *Anthropological Theory* 8 (2008), 255–77; and Coleman, *Hacker, Hoaxer, Whistleblower, Spy: The Many Faces of Anonymous* (New York: Verso, 2014). See also David Golumbia, "Cyberlibertarianism: The Extremist Foundations of 'Digital Freedom,'" talk delivered at Clemson University, September 5, 2013, available via his blog, *Uncomputing*, uncomputing.org.
36 Richard Stallman, *Free Software, Free Society* (Boston: Free

Software Foundation, 2002), 17.

37 Bill Gates, "An Open Letter To Hobbyists," *Homebrew Computer Club Newsletter* 2:1 (Mountain View, California: Homebrew Computer Club, January 1976), 2.

38 Nadia Eghbal, *Roads and Bridges: The Unseen Labor Behind Our Digital Infrastructure*, Ford Foundation, July 14, 2016.

39 Gavin Mueller, *Media Piracy in the Cultural Economy: Intellectual Property Under Neoliberal Restructuring* (New York: Routledge, 2019), 64.

40 Trevor Merriden, *Irresistible Forces: The Business Legacy of Napster and the Growth of the Underground Internet* (Mankato, MN: Capstone Publishers, 2001), 5.

41 See Kevin Driscoll, "Social Media's Dial-Up Ancestor: The Bulletin Board System," *IEEE Spectrum*, October 24, 2016, spectrum.ieee.org.

42 Humanaesfera, "A Social History of the Internet," *Intransigence* 3 (October 2018).

43 Media historian Michael Stevenson locates a slightly earlier origin of the informatization of the web, in the way that the hacker news aggregator *Slashdot* automated its editorial functions. See Stevenson, "Slashdot, Open News and Informed Media: Exploring the Intersection of Imagined Futures and Web Publishing Technology," in *New Media, Old Media: A History and Theory Reader*, 2nd ed., eds. Wendy H.K. Chun, Anna Watkins Fisher, and Thomas Keenan (London: Routledge, 2015), 616–30.

44 Tim O'Reilly, "What Is Web 2.0?," *O'Reilly Media*, September 30, 2005, oreilly.com.

45 Ibid.

46 Mark Andrejevic, "Surveillance in the Digital Enclosure," *Communication Review* 10:4 (2007), 295–317.

47 Shoshana Zuboff, "Big Other: Surveillance Capitalism and the Prospects of an Information Civilization," *Journal of Information Technology* 30 (2015), 75.

48 Ibid., 80–1.

49 Maxigas, "Hackers against Technology: Critique and Recuperation in Technological Cycles," *Social Studies of Science* 47:6 (2017), 850–1.

50 Matthew Belvedere, "AI Will Obliterate Half of All Jobs, Starting with White Collar, Says Ex-Google China President," *CNBC*, November 13, 2017, cnbc.com.

51 Jon Agar, *The Government Machine: A Revolutionary History of the Computer* (Cambridge, MA: MIT Press, 2003).

52 Virginia Eubanks, *Automating Inequality: How High-Tech Tools Profile, Police, and Punish the Poor* (New York: St. Martin's Press, 2018), 16.

53 Ibid., 82.

54 Ibid., 62.

55 Frank Pasquale, "Secret Algorithms Threaten Rule of Law," *MIT Technology Review*, June 1, 2017, technologyreview.com.

56 Cathy O'Neil, *Weapons of Math Destruction: How Big Data Increases Inequality and Threatens Democracy* (New York: Broadway Books, 2017), 95.

57 Alexandra Mateescu and Madeline Clare Elish, *AI in Context: The Labor of Integrating New Technologies*, report, *Data and Society*, January 30, 2019, 10.

58 Ibid., 49.

59 Brian Merchant, "Why Self-Checkout Is and Has Always Been the Worst," *Gizmodo*, March 7, 2019.

60 Michael Palm, *Technologies of Consumer Labor: A History of Self-Service* (New York: Routledge, 2016).

61 Rene Chun, "The Banana Trick and Other Acts of Self-Checkout Thievery," *Atlantic*, March 2018.

62 Ivan Illich, "Shadow-Work," *Philosophica* 26:2 (1980), 8.

63 Craig Lambert, *Shadow Work: The Unseen, Unpaid Jobs That Fill Your Day* (Berkeley: Counterpoint, 2015), 110.

64 Atul Gawande, "Why Doctors Hate Their Computers," *New Yorker*, November 12, 2018.

65 Sean Coughlan, "Surgery Students 'Losing Dexterity to Stitch Patients,'" *BBC News*, October 30, 2018.

66 Jathan Sadowski, "Potemkin AI," *Real Life*, August 6, 2018, reallifemag.com

67 Astra Taylor, "The Automation Charade," *Logic* 5, 2018, logicmag.io.

68 Stephanie Olsen, "ReCaptcha: Reusing Your 'Wasted' Time Online," *CNET*, July 16, 2008, cnet.com.

69 Mary L. Gray and Siddharth Suri, *Ghost Work: How to Stop Silicon Valley from Building a New Global Underclass* (Boston: Houghton Mifflin Harcourt, 2019).

70 Dave Lee, "Why Big Tech Pays Poor Kenyans to Teach Self-Driving Cars," *BBC News*, November 3, 2018, bbc.com.

71 Sarah O'Connor, "How to Manage the Gig Economy's Growing Global Jobs Market," *Financial Times*, October 30, 2018, ft.com.

72 Ian Bogost, "Why Nothing Works Anymore," *Atlantic*, February 23, 2007, theatlantic.com.

73 Nolen Gertz, *Nihilism and Technology* (London: Rowman & Littlefield International, 2018), 3.

74 Jeanette Purvis, "Why Using Tinder Is So Satisfying," *Washington Post*, February 14, 2017, washingtonpost.com.

75 "About Tinda Finger," Tinda Finger official website, tinda-finger .com.

76 Rana Foroohar, "Year in a Word: Techlash," *Financial Times*, December 16, 2018, ft.com.

77 Chris Weller, "Silicon Valley Parents Are Raising Their Kids Tech-Free—and It Should Be a Red Flag," *Business Insider*, February 18, 2018, businessinsider.com.

78 Ben Tarnoff and Moira Weigel, "Why Silicon Valley Can't Fix Itself," *Guardian*, May 3, 2018, theguardian.com.

79 Trebor Scholz, *Uberworked and Underpaid: How Workers Are Disrupting the Digital Economy* (Cambridge, UK: Polity, 2016), 159.

80 Andrew Perrin, "Americans Are Changing Their Relationship with Facebook," *Pew Research Center*, September 5, 2018, pewresearch.org.

81 Andrew Perrin and Monica Anderson, "Share of US Adults Using Social Media, including Facebook, Is Mostly Unchanged Since 2018," Pew Research Center, April 10, 2019, pewresearch.org.

82 Sirin Kale, "Logged Off: Meet the Teens Who Refuse to Use Social Media," *Guardian*, August 29, 2018, theguardian.com.

83 Simon Parkin, "The Youtube Stars Heading for Burnout: 'The Most Fun Job Imaginable Became Deeply Bleak,'" *Guardian*, September 8, 2018, theguardian.com.

84 Frauke Zeller and David Harris Smith, "What a Hitchhiking Robot Can Teach Us about Automated Coworkers," *Harvard Business Review*, December 18, 2014, hbr.org.

85 Ibid.

86 Adam Gabbat, "Hitchbot's Decapitators Avoided Capture by the Hitchhiking Android's Cameras," *Guardian*, August 3, 2015, theguardian.com.

87 Martin Wolf, *The Rise of the Robots: Technology and the Threat of a Jobless Future* (New York: Basic Books, 2015).

88 Paris Martineau, "Someone Covered This Robot Security Guard in Barbecue Sauce and Bullied It Into Submission," *New York Magazine*, December 15, 2017, nymag.com.

89 Simon Romero, "Wielding Rocks and Knives, Arizonans Attack Self-Driving Cars," *New York Times*, December 31, 2018, nytimes.com.

90 Matt Beane, "Robo-Sabotage Is Surprisingly Common," *MIT Technology Review*, August 4, 2015, technologyreview.com.

91 Nick Statt, "Amazon Says Fully Automated Shipping Warehouses Are at Least a Decade Away," *Verge*, May 1, 2019, theverge.com.

92 Josh Dzieza, "'Beat the Machine': Amazon Warehouse Workers Strike to Protest Inhumane Conditions," *Verge*, Jul 16, 2019, theverge.com.

93 Sam Adler-Bell, "Surviving Amazon," *Logic*, August 3, 2019, logicmag.io.

Conclusion

1 Leigh Phillips and Michal Rozworski, *The People's Republic of Walmart* (London and New York: Verso, 2019); Aaron Bastani, *Fully Automated Luxury Communism* (London and New York: Verso, 2018).

2 Catherine Ruetschlin and Sean McElwee, "The Big Influence of the Big Box," *American Prospect*, December 3, 2014, prospect.org

3 Julie Turkewitz, "A Boom Time for the Bunker Business and Doomsday Capitalists," *New York Times*, August 13, 2019, nytimes.com. My own roundup of some of these tendencies can be found in "Bad and Bourgeois," *Jacobin*, February 5, 2017, jacobinmag.com.

4 Carl Honoré, *In Praise of Slowness: Challenging the Cult of Speed* (New York: HarperCollins, 2005), 14.

5 "Why Slow?," World Institute of Slowness official website, theworldinstituteofslowness.com.

6 Honoré, *In Praise of Slowness*, 16.

7 Nick Dyer-Witheford, *Cyber-Proletariat: Global Labour in the Digital Vortex* (London: Pluto, 2015).

8 A.W. Geiger, "How Americans See Automation and the Workplace in 7 Charts," Pew Research Center, April 8, 2019, pewresearch.org.

9 Aaron Smith, "Public Attitudes woward Computer Algorithms," Pew Research Center, November 16, 2018, pewresearch.org.

10 Carl Benedkt Frey, *The Technology Trap: Capital, Labor, and Power in the Age of Automation* (Princeton: Princeton University Press, 2019), 291.

11 Ibid., 290–1.

12 Marc Bergen, "Google Engineers Refused to Build Security Tool to Win Military Contracts," *Bloomberg*, June 21, 2018, bloomberg.com.

13 Nitasha Tiku, "Why Tech Worker Dissent Is Going Viral," *Wired*, June 29, 2018, wired.com.

14 Jillian D'Onfro, "Google Walkouts Showed What the New Tech Resistance Looks Like, with Lots of Cues from Union Organizing," *CNBC*, November 3, 2018, cnbc.com.

15 Julia Carrie Wong, "Google Staff Condemn Treatment of Temp Workers in 'Historic' Show of Solidarity," *Guardian*, April 2, 2019, theguardian.com.

16 *The Ecomodernist Manifesto*, published by the Breakthrough Institute, is a paradigmatic example offering technological solutions to the crisis. As Bruno Latour put it in his critique of the document, "They seriously believe that nothing will happen to them and that they may continue forever, just as before." See Latour, "Fifty Shades of Green," presentation to the panel on modernism at the Breakthrough Dialog, June 2015, Sausalito, California.

17 Alyssa Battistoni, "Living, Not Just Surviving," *Jacobin*, August 15, 2017, jacobinmag.com.

18 Troy Vettese, "To Freeze the Thames," *New Left Review* 111 (May/June 2018).

19 Serge LaTouche, *Farewell to Growth* (New York: Polity, 2010), 56.

20 Ibid., 14.

21 Giorgios Kallis et al., "Research on Degrowth," *Annual Review of Environment and Resources* 43 (2018), 296.

22 LaTouche, *Farewell*, 68.

23 Andrew Russell and Lee Vinsel, "Let's Get Excited about Maintenance," *New York Times*, July 22, 2017, nytimes.com.

24 "About Us," Maintainers official website, themaintainers.org.

25 Shannon Mattern, "Minimal Maintenance," *Lapsus Lima*, October 2, 2019, lapsuslima.com.

26 Elsewhere, Mattern reminds us that maintenance also includes a feminist tradition critical of such work. See "Maintenance and Care," *Places Journal*, November 2018, placesjournal.org.

27 Jason Koebler, "Why American Farmers Are Hacking Their Tractors with Ukrainian Firmware," *Motherboard*, March 21, 2017, vice.com.

28 Nathan Proctor, "Right to Repair Is Now a National Issue," *Wired*, April 1, 2019, wired.com.

29 "About," Restart Project official website, therestartproject.org.

30 Louis Althusser, "Contradiction and Overdetermination," in *For Marx*, trans. Ben Brewster (New York: Vintage, 1970), 99.

31 Stuart Hall, "Signification, Representation, Ideology: Althusser and the Post-Structuralist Debates," *Critical Studies in Mass Communication* 2:2 (June 1985), 95.

32 Althusser, "Contradiction and Overdetermination," 100.

33 Karl Marx, letter to Domela Nieuwenhuis, February 22, 1881, in *Marx and Engels Correspondence*, trans. Donna Torr (New York: International Publishers, 1968).

Index

Ludd, Ned, 10, 12–13, 15
"Luddite confessionals," 12
Luddites/Luddism: as assuming
  mythic character, 12;
  characteristics of, 129; as
  composing themselves as a class,
  16; and degrowth, 132; free
  software as example of, 107;
  Green Luddism, 131; hackers
  as, 105–6; history as not being
  kind to, 11–12; large shadow
  of, 13; machine breaking by, 11;
  as manifesting itself differently
  according to context, 134–5;
  and Marxism, 5; Marx on,
  24; as not altogether pointless,
  14; origins of, 4–5, 10–11;
  policies of, 130; as popular, 129;
  possibility of success of, 160;
  privacy applications as another
  kind of Luddite technology, 111;
  rhetorical power of, 12; secrecy
  and solidarity of, 17; turning
  Marxists into, 5; as ultimately
  unsuccessful, 14; as way to
  challenge changes in technical
  composition of capital, 129
Lukács, Georg, 47–8
Luxemburg, Rosa, 38–9

machine breaking: as form of
  solidarity, 17; hitchBOT, 123–4;
  as ingredient in roiling stew
  of class composition, 103; by
  Luddites, 11, 13, 14–15, 17;
  motivations for, 15; as practice
  of political composition, 16; by
  Soviet workers, 51; as viewed
  by nineteenth-century bourgeois
  observers, 18
machine learning, 117, 118
machines: Marx's theory of, 21–2;
  Technocracy's embrace of, 46
MacKenzie, Donald, 20
Macleod, Iain, 61, 63
Magnitogorsk manufacturing center
  (Soviet Union), 50, 51
Maintainers, 132–3
Malcolm X, 78

Mandel, Ernest, 80–1
manufacturing, location of, 75
March on Washington for Jobs
  and Freedom, 77
Marcuse, Herbert, 69–70, 71–2,
  73
Marx, Karl, 5, 13, 14, 16, 18–24,
  28, 29, 55, 135–6
Marxists/Marxism: on confronting
  restructuring of behavior, 110;
  Flynn's analysis of sabotage
  and, 43; and Luddites/Luddism,
  5; on technology, 4; theory of
  social and technological change,
  72; as theory of struggle, 29
Mason, Paul, 21
Mattern, Shannon, 133
Maxigas, 111
McNamara, Robert, 94
medical profession, effect of digital
  shadow work on, 116–17
Merchant, Brian, 115
Microsoft, 108, 130
military-industrial complex, 63
Mills, Albion, 13
Modi, Narendra, 2
Mohandesi, Salar, 16
Monopoly Capitalism (Sweezy and
  Baran), 80
More Work for Mother (Cowan),
  87
Morgan, Katie, 123
Morris, William, 26–8, 29
Murray, Patrick, 23
Musk, Elon, 1–2

Napster, 107–8
natural geo-engineering, 132
Ned Ludd and Queen Mab
  (Linebaugh), 17
Negri, Antonio, 20, 21
neo-Luddite movement, 12
News and Letters, 70, 71, 72
Newton, Huey, 82–3
New York Times, "Guaranteed
  Income Asked for All, Employed
  or Not," 80
Nieuwenhuis, Ferdinand Domela,
  135–6

Noble, David F., 46, 63, 75
Nolan, Mary, 54
Northrup, Herbert, 80
NYU student protests, 96

Office of Scientific Research and
    Development (US), 64
office work, deskilling of, 98–9
Old Mole (student publication), 96
One-Dimensional Man (Marcuse),
    69–70, 71–2
O'Neil, Gerard K., 1
O'Neill, Cathy, 114
operaismo (workerism), 61
Operation Igloo White, 95
O'Reilly, Tim, 109, 110
Osborne, Michael A., 58
Owen, William, 61–2

Pacific Maritime Association, 75
Palm, Michael, 115
Palmer, Bryan, 34
Panzieri, Raniero, 15
participatory media, 109
Pasquale, Frank, 114
passive resistance, 101
Paterson silk mill (New Jersey),
    strike at, 43
Pauling, Linus, 78
People's Republic of Walmart
    (Phillips and Rozworski), 127
Perrot, Michelle, 24–5
personal computing, software for,
    106
Pew Research Center: poll about
    restriction of automation,
    129–30; report on social media
    use, 123
Phillips, Leigh, 127
Philosophy of Manufactures (Ure),
    18
Pinker, Steven, 3
plantation economy, slave
    insurgency in, 17–18
Plekhanov, Georgi, 39
political composition, machine
    breaking as practice of, 16
Potemkin AI, 117
Poulantzas, Nicos, 98–9

*The Power of Women and the
    Subversion of the Community*
    (James and Dalla Costa), 86
predictive analytics, 114
predictive policing (PredPol), 114
Processed World (magazine), 101–4
"producerist" vision of society, 25
production: automobile production,
    57; capital as controlling process
    of, 22; capitalist mode of, 27, 36,
    37, 38, 39, 40, 47, 48, 51; ceding
    control of to management, 66;
    cultural production, 52, 53;
    exploitative models of, 128;
    expulsion of workers from
    process of, 68; forces of, 20, 23;
    introduction of machines into
    processes of, 59; location of, 75;
    Luddism as rejecting production
    for production's sake, 129;
    machines used to increase
    production under capitalism, 26;
    management as seeking to wrest
    control of away from machinists,
    64; Marx as distinguishing
    between social relations of and
    technical relations of, 19–20;
    military values as impacting,
    63–4; new forms of as requiring
    new forms of society, 37;
    socialist production, 36, 49;
    speeding up of process of, 67;
    Taylorized production, 48; of
    things and of ideas, 39
progress, enemies of, 3
"progressophobia," 3
Project Maven, 130
proletarian struggle, Marx as
    cartographer of, 24
Proletkult initiatives, 48–9
proscience left, 4
Proudhon, Pierre-Joseph, 24
punch cards, and student
    movements (1960s), 93–4
Purvis, Jeanette, 120
Pynchon, Thomas, 12

Randolph, A. Philip, 77
Rautenstrauch, Walter, 45

United Mine Workers of America
(UMWA), 66–7, 68
United States: destruction of
machines and factories in, 13;
Industrial Workers of the World
(IWW), 41, 42, 44, 46; Johnson-
Forest Tendency, 67, 68; Office
of Scientific Research and
Development, 64; Taft-Hartley
Act (1947), 66; unruliness of
workforce in, 64; *See also* US Air
Force; US Supreme Court
universal basic income, 46
University of Wisconsin student
protests, 96
unplugging, 6
Ure, Andrew, 18
US Air Force, as leading way on
electronic battlefield, 95
user behavior, subsumption of, 111
user data, 109
US Supreme Court, ruling on
computer code, 106
utopians, 21, 28, 29–30, 49, 50,
104

Veblen, Thorstein, 43–4, 45
Vercellone, Carlo, 20
Vettese, Troy, 132
Vietnam War, electronic battlefield
of, 94–5
Vinsel, Lee, 133
Von Ahn, Luis, 118

Wages for Housework movement,
86
Wajcman, Judith, 90
Walmart, as swallowing the globe,
128
Warren, Elizabeth, 134
waterfront workers, culture of,
73–7

Watertown Arsenal
(Massachusetts), strike at, 31,
34–5
The Wealth of Nations (Smith), 34
weaver insurrection, that led to
founding of Luddism, 10–11,
25
Web 2.0, 109–10
Weigel, Moira, 122
Weir, Stan, 73, 74–5
Westmoreland, William, 94
White, Lee C., 79–80
white collar proletariat, 98–9
"Why Are There Still So Many
Jobs?" (Autor), 59
Wiener, Norbert, 64, 65–6
Willhelm, Sidney, 81–2
Williams, Alex, 58
Wilmer, Clive, 26
Wobblies, 41, 43, 44, 56
Wolf, Martin, 124
work: attractive work, 27; debate
over, 5; deskilling of office work,
98–9; ghost work, 118, 119;
shadow work, 116
workers' movements: growth, 36–7;
philosophies of, 35–6
working class, defined, 16
"The Work of Art in the Age of
Mechanical Reproduction"
(Benjamin), 52
World Wide Web, 107, 108
Wright, Steve, 102
Wu, Tim, 6

YouTube, 123

Zeller, Frauke, 123–4
Zerowork, 16
Zuboff, Shoshana, 99–100, 101,
103, 110
Zuckerberg, Mark, 2